19·12·74   (12)

AUTHOR	CLASS
HEWITT, L.	749·22✗
TITLE	**No.**
Chippendale and all the rest	45009117/

Chippendale
and All the Rest

CHIPPENDALE
AND

Linda Hewitt

Illustrations by Robert G. Hewitt

ALL THE REST

*Some Influences on Eighteenth-Century
English Furniture*

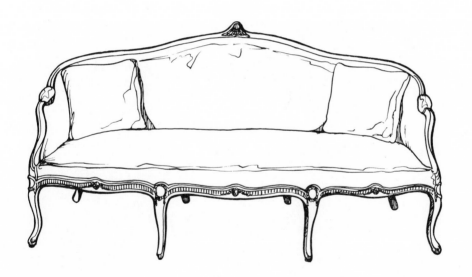

SOUTH BRUNSWICK AND NEW YORK: A. S. BARNES AND COMPANY
LONDON: THOMAS YOSELOFF LTD

© 1974 by A. S. Barnes and Co., Inc.

A. S. Barnes and Co., Inc.
Cranbury, New Jersey 08512

Thomas Yoseloff Ltd
108 New Bond Street
London W1Y OQX, England

Library of Congress Cataloging in Publication Data

Hewitt, Linda, 1940–
    Chippendale and all the rest.

    Bibliography: p. 141/
    1. Furniture, English. 2. Chippendale, Thomas,
1718–1779. 3. Cabinet-workers—England. I. Title.
NK2529.H49   749.2′2   73–6386
ISBN 0–498–01188–7

450091171

PRINTED IN THE UNITED STATES OF AMERICA

This book
is dedicated
to
our friend
Marjorie Royce,
the
original inspiration

Contents

Acknowledgments

At this point, it is customary for the author to thank the various people and institutions who aided her in the research or preparation of her work. My debt is too widespread to admit of such a luxurious undertaking. To all of those scholars, therefore, whose original researches make possible works like this, I can only express my most sincere gratitude and hope that my bibliographical notes will indicate to whom the most gratitude is due.

I also wish to thank Dr. David Wells, in whose graduate seminar at Georgia State University I began work on this book. Dr. Wells, whose interest and encouragement have benefited many students, is one of those rare historians who truly appreciates and understands the importance of the "small" and personal aspects of history.

Finally and most obviously, thanks are due to Chippendale and all the rest, without whose efforts there would be no reason for this book.

Atlanta, Georgia
January, 1972

Linda Hewitt

Introduction

Anyone who is interested in eighteenth-century English furniture can easily see what it looks like. Museums the world over possess outstanding examples, and many great and some only impressive English houses boast room after room of the furniture that was a product of what social historian John Gloag has termed "The Magnificent Century." Magazines concerned with perpetuating appreciation of man's more-sublime creations annually devote dozens of their pages to measuring, describing, picturing, discovering, and authenticating the designs and works of Messrs. Kent, Chippendale, Adam, *et al*. Countless books have appeared in the last half-century which analyze, identify, and often deify these craftsmen and their productions.

This book is aimed at the same target as its numerous predecessors: the collector, connoisseur, or student, but with a difference. Rather than providing provenance for a specific craftsman's works or debating the superiority of Adam to Kent, I hope to provide the reader with a short, readable, reasonably comprehensive history of the influences that affected furniture design and production in eighteenth-century England.

The English craftsman's successful assimilation of the influences abroad during this invigorating time is manifest as one views his dining tables, dressing tables, game tables, side tables, tripod tables, shaving tables, writing tables, library tables, drum tables, silver tables, tea tables, pier tables, console tables, sofa tables, breakfast tables, arm chairs, side chairs, hall chairs, library chairs, elbow chairs, close stools, benches, settees, garden seats, window seats, sofas, couches, beds, desks, chests, commodes, sideboards, basin stands, candle stands, bookcases, cabinets, clothes presses, china cases, clock cases, bureau cabinets, secrétaire cabinets, hanging shelves, pedestals, brackets, knife boxes, pier glasses, girandoles, mantels, fire screens, book wheelbarrows, and many other pieces. (One begins to think that a fertile imagination in devising names was a not inconsiderable influence!)

England in the eighteenth century saw rapid and continual change in every area of life, and the function and form of furniture matched the pace. From Palladian to rococo to Chinese to Gothic to neoclassical, one fashion succeeded another, and the furniture craftsmen catered to and created this taste for the ever different. Nevertheless, whatever exotic turns contemporary taste took, eighteenth-century English craftsmen sought proportion and balance in their creations. In doing so, as historian J. H. Plumb remarks, "The great masters . . . immortalized themselves and their time."

A piece of furniture for every purpose in one distinct style or another was their achievement as the cabinet-makers reflected the national unwillingness to accept the status quo. Wide experimentation was both result and cause of this restlessness until, finally, the English cabinetmakers became so proficient that the best of their work remains unsurpassed.

No work of art, least of all good furniture which must be useful as well as aesthetically satisfying, is born in a vacuum. Furniture is shaped quite literally by many forces: the tenor of the times, economic conditions, restrictions imposed by availability of raw materials, developments in other areas of art, the psychic and physical needs of patrons, the introduction of foreign modes, and the imagination and capability of the craftsmen themselves. Eighteenth-century English furniture profited greatly by the interaction of these influences, for it was first and foremost a product of its time.

I

The Tenor of the Times

In retrospect, the casual observer might see in eighteenth-century England a time of studied grace, calm sophistication, and exquisite taste. This view would not be entirely false, but the world beyond the elegantly draped windows of the London townhouses and the great country estates was undergoing rapid and often disturbing change.

As the population increased, so did crime and other social problems. As some men grew immensely richer, others knew increasing poverty.

Population, the basic fabric of the nation, remained stable in the first half of the century. By 1750 it numbered only six million, less than one-third that of France, but by 1800 there were nine million Englishmen.

The problems created by the population expansion were complicated by developments in farming and industry. The growth of the factory system undercut the importance of the family as a basic unit of production, meaning that almost all members of families in the lower economic classes, including children, had to seek employment outside the home. Many artisans found that their methods could not compete with the new technology. Advanced farming techniques required capital and more land than remained to many small farmers after the enclosures of the century.

15

This was generally a time of genuine and stable prosperity. The over-all wealth of the nation increased quickly, but this well being was not shared equally by all Englishmen. As a result, the social upheavals that usually accompany periods of transition did not spare this century.

Those citizens who were in no position to profit from the burgeoning prosperity found that they must shift as best they could. While wealthy industrialists and the landed gentry ordered furniture to fill the great houses that were meant to last forever, the poor were of necessity concerned with survival until the next day. To survive, they developed a mobility that seems impossible today. For some poor people, mobility meant regular travels about the land to aid with harvesting or to do odd work wherever it might be had. For others, mobility simply meant leaving the inhospitable countryside for the cities, especially London.

The lure of the city resulted in a concentration of large hordes of ill-educated, untrained, undernourished, inadequately housed, and generally discontented poor people. Fear rather than understanding was the reaction of the more stable and prosperous members of society. Crimes against property mounted steadily, and those persons who were convicted of stealing property, even food, often found conviction followed by a trip to the gallows amidst a carnival-like setting. Respectable citizens could watch the proceedings with a thrill of virtuous horror, and prostitutes and pickpockets plied their trades with scant chance of detection.

The conditions in which the poor lived engendered a hopelessness that the unfortunate were quick to drown in drink. Between 1750 and 1751, for example, eleven million gallons of spirits were consumed by only six million Englishmen. The eighteenth-century poor were not prone to suffer their miserable lot with only the nebulous consolation of virtue.

These years were no time for the weak of body, mind, or stomach. Enteric fevers were special menaces for the crowded city populations. London's mortality rate exceeded its birth rate for much of the century; and its growth was due to the influx of new indigents from the country, themselves particularly susceptible to disease because of inadequate diet, clothing, and shelter. The weak in mind fared no better. Bedlam drew many fashionable sight-seers who came to gape and giggle at its manacled lunatics. Even amusements were often coarse and cruel. Bear and bull baiting and cockfights still had enthusiastic followers in all classes.

Life for many Englishmen was more pitiful than picturesque, more hard than handsome in these eventful years. It is always painful to be hungry, but more painful in a society which condemns hunger, and difficult to be weak in a world which rewards only the strong. A robust era of immense vitality and exciting possibilities, eighteenth-century England could be both unfeeling and cruel.

Perhaps the almost-morbid obsession of so many propertied men of this time with family mansions and their furnishings was at least partly a reaction to the less-attractive aspects of the age. Certainly the relatively frantic pace of life made such people treasure the peace and serenity represented by the insular life style that they enjoyed. Order and beauty might not exist in the world at large, but the well-to-do Englishman could create for himself a private world in which his least whim of taste could be indulged to give him whatever sort of individual existence he preferred.

The domestic problems that disturbed so many Englishmen were not England's only or even major concern. Committed to exploration and colonization and eager to reap the trading profits that followed, England fought France throughout the century for world-wide commercial and colonial supremacy. In war after war and battle after battle in faraway places whose names most Englishmen could not even pronounce, England solidified its international position to emerge as the world's leading imperial power at the close of the century. Only the successful American revolt interrupted the nation's steady acquisition of colonies and trading rights. The growth of the British Navy kept pace with these ever-increasing imperial possessions.

As displaced farmers grumbled and British sailors saw the world, British scientists sat in coffee houses and exchanged ideas and listened to lectures by especially illustrious members of their calling. This interchange of theories soon became formalized in societies with the avowed aim of promoting still more discoveries. It was in this century that science ceased to be a private hobby and became an activity with military and economic possibilities interesting to both state and society. Intellectuals marveled at scientific progress and saw in it the solution for many problems, not the tool that would make possible the construction of an even more materialistic and problem-ridden era.

One highly visible and usable result of the collaboration between science and daily needs transformed the face of much of the English countryside. Bridges, roads, and aqueducts multiplied in numbers and gave the country a much-improved transportation system. The modernized transportation network made more practical the shipment of goods to every corner of the land.

The government that ruled this changing land was a monarchy controlled by a stable aristocracy, with Parliament holding the purse strings. The Hanoverians, descendants of the early Stuarts, came to the English throne in 1714 upon the death of Queen Anne, the last Stuart monarch. George I spoke no English, could barely be bothered by English concerns, and scandalized the court by his open patronage of his extremely unattractive mistresses. Royalty should, his court felt, exercise either good taste or discretion in such affairs, but George seemed incapable of either. George II, who at least progressed to broken English, got on with his subjects little better than he did with his irascible father. George III, thoroughly English and painfully respectable, meant well but exercised poor judgment in his choice of advisers and ministers. Political infighting, usually playing off one member of the royal family against another, was characteristic of the court. This game was made easier by the one quality that most of the Hanoverians shared—the inability to tolerate one's nearest relations.

Hanoverian family discord and political ineffectiveness were accompanied by an almost-total disinterest in the arts. With rare exceptions, the members of the House of Hanover failed to provide a strong cultural axis for either the nation at large or the court circle itself.

If, as the saying goes, poor government and poor people are always with us, so are the rich; and many Englishmen found themselves enjoying that enviable state in the eighteenth century. Wealth came from the new factories, from the radically improved agricultural methods and stock-breeding techniques, from imperial possessions, from court office, and from marriage. That most of the wealth was made through the exploitation of some other group of people did not concern the newly prosperous overmuch. The slaves upon whose labor much of the imperial wealth depended were, after all, far away. Those small farmers who were forced off the land by the enclosures were closer to home and might, perhaps, be people that one knew; but overlooking them too was not difficult for men blinded by the light that riches always cast. Bribery and corruption had always been part of court life. The children employed in the factories and mines were better off there than begging in the streets. A man might as well marry a rich woman as a poor one. The rationalizations were many and, it must be admitted, not always baseless.

All the same, even allowing for more-delicate modern sensibilities about child labor, slavery, starvation, bribery, and the like, the eighteenth century at times appears most unappealing. It was materialistic

—perhaps the first age of materialism—and harsh to rejects from its system.

It is tempting but misleading to judge another time by the ideals of our own. We should see eighteenth-century England in its proper perspective, as a nation with an exceptionally enlightened government for its time, with leaders who sometimes showed remarkable political and social insight, with a vigorous aristocracy that tempered its quest for wealth and status with learning and wit, and with a people alive with a keen sense of experimentation. It was a time of great optimism for the future.

Members of the landed and commercial aristocracy were the chief beneficiaries of the new prosperity, prompting them to acquire knowledge that would enable them to live as their own self-esteem demanded. They spent a healthy share of their fortunes to create a setting appropriate to their position and aspirations. If we describe their efforts as exercises in ego gratification, we must also admit that at least they paid themselves the compliment of self-respect and sought the best of music, literature, art, architecture, and furniture.

In any age, people—whether an individual family or a nation—participate in many spheres of activity. They love, they fear, they hope, they war, they live. To themselves and to their fellow men they present an image, deliberate or accidental. The way in which those persons not bound by poverty or ignorance choose to live from day to day, that is, the physical framework that they create for their daily comfort and subsistence, is perhaps one of the most significant indicators of their civilization.

In this respect, the aristocracy of eighteenth-century England provided a creditable reflection of their time. Warts they may have had, but—more important—they also had an undeniable talent for successful living that makes them appealing even today.

Their most tangible legacy is the substantial body of architecture that they erected throughout England and filled with the exuberantly designed furniture that is the subject of this book. This magnificent furniture remains a flattering reflection of what A. E. Richardson has characterized as the "calm individualism" of the pacesetters of the age.

2

Chippendale and Who Else?

Any writer interested in English furniture and its creators is tempted to call the years between the accession of Queen Anne and the Regency the Chippendale century, so ubiquitous has been the great self-advertiser's influence since he departed the stylish world he had spent his life furnishing and decorating. Antique dealers today are quick to point with pride to any piece remotely "Chippendalish." Hostesses in the Governor's Palace at Williamsburg breathlessly attribute an impressive bookcase to the master. Auctioneers are prone to murmur "Chinese Chippendale" over anything with blind fretwork. Manufacturers of modern reproduction pieces like to call anything with curved legs Chippendale.

Without disparaging Thomas Chippendale or revoking the charter of his widespread if unorganized fan club, it is only fair to point out that there were literally hundreds of cabinetmakers, upholsterers, and furniture designers working in London during the century to supply the wealthy with furnishings for their townhouses and country mansions. London was the center of the furniture business, and the demand by society for fashion meant that the clientele who could afford to patronize London makers and designers did so.

Many of these cabinetmakers and designers live for us only through their elegantly designed tradesmen's cards proclaiming the goods and services that they were prepared to offer as well as their ability to do so "in the neatest Manner" or "most Superb style" and "at the most reasonable Rates." Probably most of them designed and crafted furniture still in existence, but giving the individual maker credit for his surviving work is usually impossible.

Had English cabinetmakers and their brethren obligingly labeled or otherwise marked their work, much confusion and disagreement over eighteenth-century furniture would not exist. In France such marking was in many cases required by law after 1741. In England the few cabinetmakers who labeled their finished work did so as an advertising gimmick. The majority of cabinetmakers, including the most fashionable, rarely used labels. Even when labels were attached to furniture, clients often scraped them off, or their location was such that the labels simply wore off so that labeled pieces are unusual. Marks other than labels were exceptions. Chairmaker firms sometimes stamped their initials on a chair's seat rail, but we usually cannot be sure of the firm or the person to whom the initials refer.

This thoughtless modesty of the eighteenth-century English cabinetmakers has given a small army of dedicated scholars the inspiration to seek out the names and personalities of these men who hitherto languished in the shadows just beyond the searchlight of attention focused on Chippendale and on the furniture that they all helped to create. Research into eighteenth-century directories, newspaper ads, tradesmen's cards, billheads, makers' labels, design books, and even contemporary works of poetry, drama, and prose has disinterred one after another of the designers and craftsmen sharing the Chippendale century.

Nonetheless, this increase of knowledge has not always made possible the definite attribution of a specific piece of furniture to a specific designer or craftsman. Attribution is traditionally allowed when the article of furniture exists with its original bill, when the furniture is marked or labeled, when a craftsman is known to have worked for a house and one of his "book pieces" is found there, or when a piece shows all the same characteristics of work and materials occurring in a definitely attributable work.

Attribution on these grounds is not infallible. Labels, for example, may have been removed from one piece and attached to another. The best cabinetmakers and designers were subject to the same design influences—foreign innovations, introduction of new materials, architectural trends, and the like—so that true originality was rare. Also, an employee of one fine cabinetmaker might find work with another, taking his unusual talents with him, so that work from both firms will show touches of the same craftsmanship. Apprentices often worked in the manner of their former masters. Even so acknowledged a master of eighteenth-century cabinetmaking techniques as William Vile, whose definitely attributable work is of such individuality and superb quality, cannot lay positive claim to all the furniture in his style because other excellent cabinetmakers worked closely with Vile and his partner John Cobb and may have made use of the same decorative devices and techniques.

Fortunately, we are not concerned so much with the specific provenance of individual articles of furniture as we are with the *kind* of craftsmen and designers who created the furniture. How did these men conduct their business? What was their training? How did they make their furniture? What was their status in the community? What influences operated on them?

Basically three groups of men were responsible for fine furniture in eighteenth-century England. There were the architects who designed furniture to complement the interiors of the houses they built for clients. There were professional designers who designed furniture for cabinetmakers and other craftsmen. Then there were the craftsmen themselves, many of whom also designed the furniture they produced.

The first English architect to coordinate the interiors of his houses was William Kent, a torchbearer of the Palladian movement that dominated English architecture after 1720. Andrea Palladio (1508–1580) was an Italian architect whose interpretation of ancient Roman architecture and whose insistence on proper form and proportion had been beautifully illustrated by his 1570 work on architecture. Dissatisfied with what they considered the decadence inherent in the baroque style of Sir John Vanbrugh and Nicholas Hawksmoor at such oversized palaces as Castle Howard and Blenheim, the English Palladians turned to what they saw as the chaste grandeur of Palladio and his seventeenth-century English disciple Inigo Jones.

Unfortunately, Palladio had not bequeathed any opinions about how his residences should be furnished to preserve that suitability which he deemed their most essential quality. Undaunted by this oversight on their hero's part, Kent and the other Palladians turned for inspiration to Inigo Jones's designs of a century before for interior doorways and chimney pieces. For furniture ornament the Palladians used the large-scale sculptural motifs such as human masks, massive scrolls, scallop shells, floral swags, and pendants so beloved of Inigo and

his pupils. These highly acceptable devices were leavened by the influence of the ostensibly less-acceptable French ornamentalists who
were then publishing their works abroad. The resulting furniture
has a distinctly baroque feel.

*Queen Anne walnut side table with shaped frieze and cabriole legs, ca. 1710.
Height: 2'4"; Length: 2'7"; Depth: 1'9".*

To enhance the opulent interiors of his clients' houses, Kent designed furniture that was bold, large, rich, ornate, and architectural.
Away from the surroundings it was meant for, Kent's furniture might
appear vulgarly overscaled, its gilded scrollwork gaudy, and its lavish
lack of comfort impractical. In the elaborately decorated and am-
bitiously proportioned rooms for which it was intended, his furniture
is as much a part of his houses as their walls.

As a rule, Kent only sketched or described his ideas, which were
then developed by a professional furniture designer for execution by
cabinetmakers. Kent's furniture reflected his wide foreign travels and
his conviction that, to be successful, furniture must be an organic part
of the interior in which it was to be used. Perhaps most important,
his furniture—as well as his interiors and certainly the picturesque
gardens he so adeptly laid out—betrayed his origin as an artist concerned with aesthetic integration and visual impact.

Kent himself worked only for a small group of very wealthy men,
for only they could afford his costly designs. Other architects, such as
the Langley brothers, adapted his designs for patrons of more modest
means.

Kent was but the first well-known architect to design furniture for his houses. Robert Adam, John Vardy, Henry Keene, Sir William Chambers, John Carter, John Yenn, Henry Holland, and Sir John Soane were some other eighteenth-century English architects who provided clients with furniture designs to coordinate interior decoration schemes.

Robert Adam, the best-known architect of this group, was also the single most-important design influence of his day. Son of a successful Scottish architect of the Palladian school, Adam drew upon the years he had spent in Italy as source material for not only the two books he published on antiquities, but also the neoclassicism that shaped his own work and proved a pivotal point in eighteenth-century architecture and design. Its forty-year infatuation with the Palladians over, England was ready in 1760 to respond to the fresh stimulus that Adam's more restrained approach heralded.

Like Kent, Adam envisioned everything in and around a house as part of the complete scheme. Also like Kent, he designed furniture that can be appreciated most fully in its original setting. Torn apart from this setting, Adam-inspired furniture often appears effeminate or even insignificant. Cabinetmakers who executed Adam's designs or who were inspired by them included some of the finest craftsmen of the day, including Thomas Chippendale, John Linnell, Samuel Norman, William France, and Samuel Beckwith.

As the years passed, English patrons tired of Adam and his contemporary followers and turned to younger architects, like Henry Holland, whose work incorporated a new breed of classicism. Holland, who worked only for the inner circle of Great Whigs, just as Adam's most important clients had been influential Tories, was married to the daughter of "Capability" Brown, the landscape architect whose notions of garden design revolutionized gardens in England and abroad.

Henry Holland shared Kent's and Adam's concern that furniture be treated as integral to the whole scheme of a house. He went to the extreme of occasionally using fitted or built-in furniture, making it literally part of a room's architecture.

Although it is true that architects did not always make good furniture designers—being less concerned with the furniture itself and the uses to which it was to be put than with the effect that it made when in place—their notion of furniture as part of a house and meant always to stay with the house marked a turning point in English design.

*George I small chest of drawers, walnut, ca. 1714–1727. Height: 2'5½";
Width: 2'6"; Depth: 1'3".*

Apart from architects, there were professional furniture designers,
men who supplied designs to cabinetmakers and other craftsmen. Some
of these designers worked in a cabinetmaker's establishment. Edward
Edwards, the artist, held such a post as a youth. Some designers combined their vocation with another. Mathew Darly, for example, was
both designer and cartoonist. Matthias Lock, who was a carver as well
as an excellent draftsman, worked in turn for both Chippendale and
James Cullen, another fine cabinetmaker. Lock has been given much
credit by some scholars for the designs in Chippendale's famous *Director*. Thomas Johnson, author of several influential pattern books,
was a free-lance carver and designer who sold his services to whichever
cabinetmaker wanted to hire him for a specific project.

Professional furniture designers performed an important function
in cabinetmaking, in that they gave craftsmen the benefit of their
knowledge of style and ornamentation. As a rule, their designs reflected current trends and did not attempt innovation.

Although architect-designers and professional furniture designers
played a definite role, the craftsmen themselves were by far the most
important factor in the production of the furniture. Some of these
craftsmen—men like Chippendale, Ince & Mayhew, Robert Manwaring, George Hepplewhite, and Thomas Sheraton—were themselves
designers of note or at least published design books. There were many

fashionable and capable craftsmen who never published their designs in book form. Their failure to publish has kept them from sharing the recognition accorded to those craftsmen who did. Only after concerted effort, for example, have we come to know much about such fine craftsmen as Gerrit Jensen, cabinetmaker to the Crown from 1689 to 1715, or John Channon, responsible for a particularly outstanding group of brass-inlaid furniture from the 1740s. Continuing research will doubtless discover more and more about lesser known craftsmen of the time.

As we survey what we know of how these successful craftsmen prepared themselves for their work and how they conducted their business, the picture—if indeed it ever existed—of the solitary genius attacking his wood in a burst of creative energy recedes into fantasy. Cabinetmaking and upholstering and the other furniture trades were businesses with organizational and personnel procedures.

Most of the men who supplied furniture and other decorative goods to royalty and the aristocracy maintained extensive operations. Daniel Bell, for example, was a successful cabinetmaker whose house, workshop, and timber supply burned in 1728. In commenting on the fire, the *Weekly Journal or British Gazetteer* noted that Bell employed "several Scores of People ever Day."

In the mid-1750s, the Sun Insurance Company made a record of Thomas Chippendale's premises, which contained:

> Counting-rooms, the dwelling house . . . Upholsterers' shop and ware room heated with a German stove: stacks for the drying of wood in the roof . . . glassroom . . . feather room with an open cockle stove . . . three-storeyed building: all cabinet-makers' shops . . . Veneering-room with feather-room over . . . Drying-room with stone floor for charcoals, containing a japanning stove and German stove; carpet-room above . . . Store-room and show-room.

Somewhat later in the century, George Seddon's workshop is said to have employed approximately four hundred people as apprentices, joiners, carvers, gilders, mirror makers, upholsterers, girdlers, and locksmiths, housing them in a large building with six wings.

Such workshops could supply merchandise in a variety of qualities and prices to order. Most shops had showrooms attached in which were displayed samples of their work that could be ordered and also some articles that could be bought on the spot. Some firms, such as Thomas Chippendale's and Ince & Mayhew's, imported and sold French furniture in their showrooms. Since so many of the best cabinetmakers and other craftsmen worked primarily to order, these showrooms were

George II walnut bureau bookcase, ca. 1725–1750. Height: 6'9"; Width: 2'11"; Depth: 13".

conducted, as their name implied, more as display areas than as sales-rooms.

John Gumley was one craftsman who early realized the importance of imaginative display rooms to attract fashionable customers. Gumley, a cabinetmaker who specialized in the manufacture of furniture that incorporated either glass or looking glass, had a Glass Gallery over the New Exchange, of which Richard Steele could proclaim in 1715 his conviction that people of whatever taste would be entertained and "well pleased" at Gumley's, "for they will have unavoidable Oppor-

tunities of seeing what they most like, in the most various and agree-
able Shapes and Positions, I mean their dear selves."

In 1705, Gumley had attacked the Bear-Garden Glass-House monopoly of looking glass. In reply Bear-Garden had accused him of
being a tradesman rather than a craftsman. Had this accusation been
true, which seems unlikely in view of Gumley's later appointment
as cabinetmaker to the Crown, he had company in the retail trade
before many years had passed. Thomas Tennant was possibly the
earliest furniture dealer, as distinct from cabinetmaker. When Surnam's, an auctioneer and apparently a kind of furniture emporium,
disposed of Tennant's household goods and stock in 1732, he was
described as "an eminent wholesale Dealer in all manner of Household Furniture," a description that the accompanying list of his extensive stock supported. By mid-century, there were a number of retail
shops that sold furniture from smaller workshops and individual
journeymen.

Few wealthy clients patronized these retail shops, preferring to order
directly from fashionable firms like Chippendale's. A few such clients
ordered furniture through a London carrier or by post, simply stating
requirements which they trusted the craftsmen to obey. Still others
would call upon the London craftsmen, and some patrons had the
craftsmen call upon them at their country estates to discuss orders.

It was not uncommon for a wealthy man to "shop" amongst several
craftsmen, seeing first one and then the other and assessing their work
and comparing their prices, a practice that was greatly simplified by the
fact that most of the top cabinetmakers were located in or near St.
Martin's Lane. The gravitational pull exerted by this area was due
in part to the location there of the Office of Works, a governmental
department responsible for the letting of many lucrative furnishing
contracts.

St. Martin's Lane and its environs must have been a more-intriguing
area before 1762, the date when street numbers replaced the more
colorful shop signs. These signs had tended to fall in one of three
categories: a symbol of the trade, an emblem of loyalty, or an amalga-
mation sign. As symbols of trade, obvious sign choices were The Chair,
The Cabinet, The Walnut Tree, The Blue Curtain, The Bed, The
Looking Glass, and the like. Familiar emblems or heraldic devices
included The King's Arms, Crown and Sceptre, The White Hart,
and The Unicorn, all of which were in wide use on signs for many
trades. The most interesting signs were those that combined a craftsman's own sign with that belonging to the former occupant of his

premises, resulting in signs like The Bull and Bedpost, The Blue Ball and Artichoke, and The Whale and Gate.

George II mahogany secrétaire press in the manner of Chippendale, ca. 1745–1760. Height: 7'6"; Width: 4"; Depth: 2'½".

No matter how large the business establishment behind the sign or number, there had to be a guiding creative power, thus we see Daniel Bell after the fire in 1728 announcing relocation of his large concern and assuring customers, "I shall be in Person to give Attention." Years later, the elegantly dressed John Cobb would stride through his workshop, issuing peremptory orders to his many workmen. The personal artistic touch of the head of the firm might not have been on all its productions, but his business acumen, foresightedness, and tact in dealing with wealthy customers formed the support without which the entire business would have collapsed.

Sometimes these businesses were sole proprietorships. Often they were partnerships. Partnerships in the furniture crafts usually combined a cabinetmaker with an upholsterer or a looking-glass-and-picture-frame maker with a gilder or some other combination where each partner supplied to the other a complementary trade. Many of the partnerships tended to be shortlived, perhaps due to the acrimony that must have been a natural by-product of the lax business principles and practices of the time. When a partnership was dissolved by death or disagreement, all the joint stock and materials was sold and the proceeds divided between the partners, who then continued in business individually or with new associates.

One notably successful partnership, formed at mid-century and lasting for fifteen years, was that of William Vile and John Cobb, probably the foremost cabinetmakers and upholsterers in England between 1755 and 1765. Vile, a cabinetmaker to the Crown, whose early work showed the baroque influence of Kent but who later developed a more refined ornament, achieved a degree of quality and individuality in his productions that sets him apart even in an age of generally high standards. Vile's partner, John Cobb, has survived to posterity primarily through J. T. Smith's contemporary description of him in *Nollekens and his Times* as "that singularly haughty character . . . perhaps one of the proudest men in England." Yet after Vile's retirement, the dapper, snobbish Cobb continued to produce fine furniture, often in the French taste featuring beautiful marquetry work.

Thomas Chippendale seems to have preferred or found it more convenient to work in a partnership. He prospered as the partner of James Rannie from 1754 to 1766, the date of Rannie's death. In 1771, he took Thomas Haig, Rannie's clerk, as a partner. Haig dealt with administration and finance and, after Chippendale's death in 1779, continued in partnership with Chippendale's son until his own retirement in 1796.

Another successful partnership was that of John Mayhew and William Ince, formed in 1759. Their *Universal System of Household Furniture,* published in folio form in 1762, was one of the best design books of the time. Like Chippendale, whose *Director* obviously furnished the inspiration for their book, Ince & Mayhew were very interested in the French styles.

Most of the fashionable firms had among their employees a full complement of the craftsmen necessary to produce the wide variety of work expected by their customers. In fact, work tended to become

George III tulip wood and walnut bombé commode, with serpentine front and shaped apron, with gilt bronze mounts, in the manner of Pierre Langlois, ca. 1770. Height: 2'11½"; Depth: 2'6"; Width: 5'2".

increasingly specialized as the century progressed, and a single piece of furniture might have been worked on by as many as three or four individual craftsmen over a period of several months.

Many workshops had designers, who usually made full-size working drawings of all but the simplest designs. From the drawings a workman would make templates, or patterns cut out of thin boards, to act as a guide in marking the wood. After the wood was marked, a carver took over. There were basically two kinds of carvers specializing in furniture production: the chair carver and the looking-glass-and-picture-frame carver. The chair carver worked on all sorts of furniture, while the looking-glass carver worked mostly on looking glasses, sconces, picture frames, gilt stands, pier tables, and marble-topped tables, i.e., upon articles that were gilded, not polished. Other specialized employees of a large workshop might include turners, japanners, marquetry workers, gilders, upholsterers, and glass grinders.

Large firms also had a number of apprentices, who paid handsomely for the privilege of learning the trade from an eminent master. At mid-century, Chippendale charged an apprenticeship fee of £20 and Giles Grendey £43. By 1762, John Channon demanded £50. When an apprentice had fulfilled his apprenticeship agreement and felt that he was sufficiently competent, he usually went into business, either alone or with a partner. Before forming their well-known partnership, for example, John Mayhew and William Ince had served apprenticeships, Mayhew with William Bradshaw and Ince with John West.

Unknown in England was the French system of promotion for craftsmen. Initiated into the furniture trade as apprentices, French-

George III satinwood cabinet, painted with figures, flowers, peacock's feathers, with a top crowned by decorated dome with carved giltwood floral ornaments, in the manner of Sheraton, ca. 1785. Height: 9'; Width: 3'10".

men then spent several years as journeymen before being permitted to pay the necessary fee and to submit a masterpiece demonstrating their ability. Only then could they be promoted to master. The English system was decidedly more casual.

Traditional methods of craftsmanship generally prevailed in the workshops throughout the century, but Sir Samuel Bentham patented woodworking machinery in the 1790s that boded changes for the future.

Just as the individual workshops were composed of craftsmen with various specialities, so the workshops themselves were often known for or specialized in making one particular kind of furniture. There were throughout the century two main divisions in the craft of furniture making: the cabinetmaker and the chairmaker. The cabinetmaker worked on furniture with drawers, on cupboards, and on tables. The chairmaker made chairs, couches, settees, and stools. Turners, who often worked as free lancers, executed turning for both chair- and cabinetmakers and even made simpler furniture to sell themselves. Upholsterers usually worked for or with chairmakers.

Apart from these main divisions, there were many less-important specialist craftsmen or firms: japanners, makers of picture frames, lacquer specialists, paperhangers, makers of papier mâché, cane specialists, and glass grinders. Most furniture craftsmen were also prepared to function as undertakers and assessors upon demand.

After the decade of 1740 to 1750, cabinet- and chairmaking and upholstering tended toward combination, as upholstering became increasingly important in furniture styles.

Specialization sometimes went to extreme lengths. Vile & Cobb, not essentially chairmakers, nonetheless in 1764 supplied to one client eight armchairs; but Selferin Alkin, an independent craftsman, carved the splats and toprails for the client. Some marquetry specialists supplied the trade at large from their own premises.

Some members of these various crafts belonged to guilds; many did not. Unlike the tightly controlled and influential French guilds, English guilds in the eighteenth century were relatively ineffective. By law, only craftsmen who lived within the city limits of London had to belong to a guild. This requirement excused from membership many prominent craftsmen who worked just outside London.

Foremost of the London furniture guilds in the eighteenth century were the Carpenters Company, the Joiners' Company, and the Upholders' Company, all dating to the fourteenth century. Both the carpenters and the joiners worked with wood, but the carpenters used nails, not glue, as the securing agent. The upholders did upholstery work. Before the seventeeth century, when furniture was not upholstered, the upholders had made bedding and hangings. It was to the Upholders Company that most eighteenth-century cabinetmakers belonged because of the increased importance of upholstery work in furniture making.

George III mahogany triple bowfront secrétaire bookcase, in the manner of Hepplewhite, ca. 1785. Height: 7'10"; Width: 5'1½".

Membership in these three companies was divided into three classes: apprentice, freeman, and liveryman. Only the liverymen governed the companies, and as a rule the other members did not attend meetings. Since the number of liverymen was small in relation to the total membership (in 1724, for example, liverymen comprised only five percent of the Joiners Company), the guilds gave most members very little sense of participation and responsibility, and consequently exerted little real influence or control.

Some form of control or at least a strong statement of ethical practices was needed, for the business morals of the time were exceedingly lax. Designs were pirated, customs officials cheated, and at least one well-known case of outright fraud perpetrated.

If the cabinetmakers were lax in their business conduct, so were their patrons who would sometimes let their accounts ride for years without making any payment. In fact, from this remove it is difficult to see how the businessmen-cabinetmakers could continue to function, unless their suppliers extended to them the same leniency which they were forced to extend to their wealthy clients.

In spite of their customers' lackadaisical paying habits, some cabinetmakers managed to accumulate sizable fortunes. This was one advantage of the loose craft and guild organization in England. The craftsmen could act as entrepreneurs, and dealers as well, because there were no guild restrictions to forbid the practice.

A good example of the wealthy craftsman was John Cobb, who died in 1778 and left extensive property, including £22,000 in stocks paying £600 a year in interest. His will reflected Cobb's inordinate pride, decreeing that the principal was to be left untouched by his heirs and only the income used so that there would always be money "to support ye Name of Cobb as a private Gentleman."

George III mahogany library table, with leather-lined top, in the manner of Henry Holland, ca. 1795. Height: 2'6½"; Width: 7'1½"; Depth: 4'1½".

A cabinetmaker who found wealth the key to social advancement was William Hallett. In 1743, Hallett bought the site of Canons, one of the most ambitious houses built in England to that date.

Built by James Gibbs for James Brydges, ninth Baron and first Duke of Chandos, Canons cost over £200,000 and was reputed to have furnishings suitable to its architectural magnificence. Hallett, in fact, early in his career had provided some of its furniture. When the Duke lost his money, Canons was put on the market. When no one bought it, the almost-new house was demolished and the materials stored. Having bought the house's site, Hallett was also present to bid on its remains when they went on the auction block in 1747. With the materials he obtained at the auction, he built a pleasant villa upon the central vaults of the old mansion. Canons was but the first of several properties that Hallett purchased, all formerly belonging to "ancient families," making Horace Walpole bemoan that trade could amalgamate these old and varied properties in one man's hands. Hallett played the role of landed gentleman to the extent of having his family's portrait painted with one of his acquisitions in the background.

Not all Georgian cabinetmakers, upholsterers, and their fellows became wealthy or even successful; and certainly not all of them attained the heights of craftsmanship so evident in the work attributed to masters like Vile, Chippendale, Channon, and Jensen. Still, the environment must have been conducive to excellence, and there was obviously room at the top for the craftsman with the necessary combination of business ability, good timing, and creativity.

Perhaps the key words in assessing the eighteenth-century London cabinetmakers as a body are competence and competition. To succeed in the aggressive business climate, the cabinetmakers had to be competent; and the high general level of competence fostered still more competition.

3
A Plethora of Publications

T*he* ambitious cabinetmakers of eighteenth-century England may be said to have shared the modern academic's dilemma of "Publish or perish!" Choosing not to risk perishing, many cabinetmakers did publish their designs, some in individual sheets, others in an elegant and expensive folio format.

The furniture craftsmen were not alone in their rush to record their ideas and achievements. Architectural publications had shown them the way; for any intelligent observer of the contemporary scene could see just how crucial a role certain key architectural design books had played in affecting public taste and attracting favorable attention to their authors.

Furniture design books had been published in Europe as early as the sixteenth century, when first German, then French and Dutch craftsmen had realized how useful such books could be in attracting buyers for their furniture. In spite of this early Continental precedent, domestic furniture design books did not appear in England until the second quarter of the eighteenth century, probably because—as Peter Ward–Jackson has indicated—they were not necessary before the demand increased in England for luxury and the highest quality in furniture.

Whether or not most of the English design books reflected highest quality was debatable; but they definitely did reflect luxury, if by that term we mean gratification of the fashionable craze for novelty and variety. Craftsmen found that a high premium was placed on being first with a design. As R. Campbell pointed out in *The London Tradesman* in 1747:

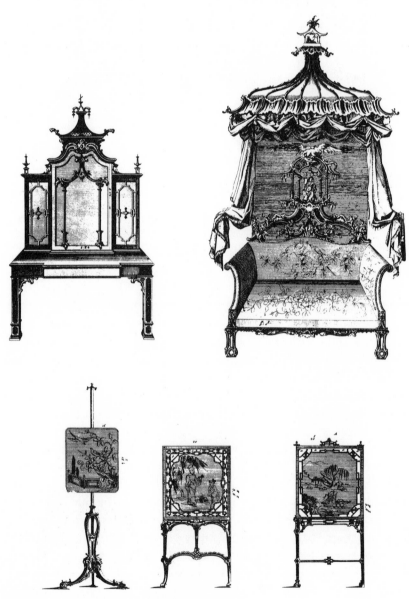

Excerpts from Chippendale's The Director

The cabinet-maker . . . requires a nice mechanic genious . . . the youth
who designs to make a figure in this branch must learn to draw, for upon
this depends the Invention of new Fashions and on that the Success of his
Business. He who first hits on any new whim is sure to make by the Invention before it becomes common in the trade.

Campbell also wrote that the cabinetmaker "that must always wait for a new Fashion till it come from Paris, or is hit upon by his Neighbor, is never likely to grow rich or eminent in this way." This observation did not keep many cabinetmakers from publishing designs that owed much to Paris, not to mention Cathay, and even to the work of fellow English craftsmen.

At first, designs for furniture appeared as a part of architectural design books, such as William Jones's *The Gentlemans or Builders Companion* (1739), which contained twenty designs for tables and mirrors. Then came designers like Matthias Lock, said to be the finest draftsman in England, who in the 1740s produced relatively small works featuring designs for specific articles of furniture. A spate of design books flooded the market in the 1750s and 1760s, some of which continued to concentrate on one article of furniture, like Mathew Darly's *A New Book of Chinese, Gothic & Modern Chairs* (1751).

It was in 1754 that the century's most important furniture pattern book appeared, the first edition of Thomas Chippendale's *The Gentleman and Cabinet-Maker's Director: Being a large Collection of the Most Elegant and Useful Designs of Household Furniture, in the Most Fashionable Taste.*

The *Director* was both an important and an interesting publication. Unlike earlier, more-modest pattern books, it proclaimed its ambitions by its size, its quality of execution, its impressive list of subscribers, the sumptuousness of its presentation, and the variety of furniture included in its pages.

For years, a scholarly dispute has continued over the true parentage of the designs in the *Director*. Were they the products of Matthias Lock and H. Copland, two designers hired by Chippendale to work on the book, or were they basically Chippendale's own insipirations?

Although it would be interesting to know just how much of Chippendale's *Director* was indeed Chippendale's, in one sense the dispute is meaningless; for the *Director* itself was not overwhelmingly original. For the most part, it simply reflected the existing interest in certain styles and motifs. The uniqueness of the *Director* lay in the range of furniture to which rococo, chinoiserie, and Gothic motifs were applied and in the care with which the furniture designs themselves were executed and engraved.

Correctly judging that a quality pattern book would more than repay its production costs by attracting wealthy and fashion-conscious customers to his establishment, Chippendale apparently spared no effort or expense in the preparation of the *Director*. In addition to the contributions of Lock and Copland, the book was fortunate to gain excellent engravers in the persons of T. and J. S. Müller and the multi-talented Mathew Darly.

At least two years in preparation, the *Director's* first edition appeared in 1754 and the second a year later. The book sold for £2.8.0, a high price for a pattern book but doubtless necessary because of the production expense. This must also have been one reason for Chippendale's obtaining such a large subscription list. It is unlikely that Chippendale personally knew all the subscribers, which included five Dukes, a Marquess, five Earls, six Barons, five Baronets or Knights, and many craftsmen in the furniture and building trades, as well as a merchant, a watchmaker, a chemist, an organ maker, and two professors of philosophy. Many of the subscribers may have been recruited by Chippendale's friends and patrons, or possibly by an appeal circulated to those persons who might logically take an interest in such a book.

The *Director's* contents included an explanation of the five orders of architecture (Tuscan, Doric, Ionic, Corinthian, and Composite), as well as designs for scores of articles of furniture. Many styles were represented, but Chippendale's integration of rococo, chinoiserie, and Gothic elements into a style which might best be termed—at least in a few examples—neofantastic was the ingredient providing the first edition's distinctive flavor. In the third edition, many of the more exotic designs disappeared, for Chippendale retained only 95 plates from the earlier editions. The 105 new plates were not radically different from the old except that they revealed a heavier dependence upon French sources for ornament, possibly revealing Chippendale's awareness of the success enjoyed by Thomas Johnson's designs in the rococo idiom.

With the enlarged third edition, the price increased to £3, but patrons who had bought the first edition could buy the new plates bound separately for £1.16.0. In spite of its relatively high price, the *Director* enjoyed a wide circulation in all of its editions, and had an undoubted influence on furniture craftsmen for many years.

That the *Director* was intended more as a businessman's advertisement to potential customers than as a craftsman's creative medium is self-evident. Whatever any critic thinks about Thomas Chippendale's credentials as a craftsman, no one can fault Thomas Chippendale, businessman. His gamble in producing the *Director* paid handsome returns. Its success is probably the primary reason for the inordinate

Excerpts from Mayhew & Ince's Universal System

amount of attention usually accorded Chippendale in eighteenth-century cultural history.

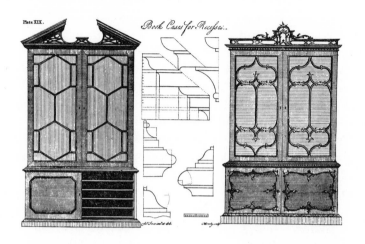

The *Director's* success had another, more-immediate effect in the avalanche of pattern books that descended upon London throughout the remainder of the century. One book obviously and directly inspired by the *Director's* reception was Ince & Mayhew's *The Universal System of Household Furniture,* published from 1759 onwards in individual sheets, then in 1762 in book form.

Opening with examples of "Ornaments for Practice," *Universal System* proceeded to show approximately three hundred designs for a wide range of furniture. As was perhaps inevitable considering the similar nature of the two books, *Universal System* resembled the *Director* in many ways. The layouts of the two were much the same; even the styles represented in *Universal System* often smacked strongly of those in the *Director.* Nonetheless, the later book is not of the same high quality.

Like Chippendale, Ince & Mayhew had hired Mathew Darly to engrave their book; but the drawings themselves lack the vigor of those in the *Director*, often appearing merely busy. Still, *Universal System* was an ambitious publication, and doubtless gave the youthful partnership a good beginning.

A design book with an entirely different purpose was William Chambers's *Designs of Chinese Buildings, Furniture, Dresses, Machines and Utensils* (1757). Chambers, unlike any of the other so-called experts on the Chinese taste, had actually been to China where he had observed the country and its inhabitants and their way of life. Totally disgusted with what European and English designers were promoting as "Chinese" motifs, Chambers—an architect who was later Robert Adam's most successful competitor—saw his book as a needed antidote to the unthinking acceptance of these rococo visions of Cathay.

Where the *Director* and *Universal System* had been directed to potential customers and Chambers's book to the arbiters of taste, Thomas Johnson meant his pattern books of the 1750s and 1760s for cabinetmaking firms. Johnson's 1758 *Collection of Designs* was probably the most exuberant flowering of the rococo in England; and Johnson, a free–lance carver and designer, hoped that it would increase his chance of employment by the large establishments.

Even the generally sluggish trade associations were not above dirtying their hands with printer's ink. The Society of Upholsterers, formed by a group of leading designers, published *Household Furniture in Genteel Taste for the year 1760,* which contained "upwards of 180 designs on 60 copper plates." Its probable aim was to garner prestige and to increase business for the trade as a whole; and since its contributors included Thomas Chippendale, Ince & Mayhew, Thomas Johnson, and Robert Manwaring, it doubtless succeeded. A second edition was subsequently published, and three years after the first edition the Society issued *Household Furniture for the year 1763.*

As mentioned earlier, producers of these design books were not always over–scrupulous in borrowing from one another. It seems especially ironic that the designer who openly criticized this practice should have been in one instance guilty of plagiarism himself. The critical designer was Robert Manwaring, and sad to say his 1766 *The Chair-Maker's Guide . . . 200 new and genteel designs* was no newer than Mathew Darly's 1751 publication *New Book of Chinese, Gothic & Modern Chairs,* from which the *Guide* was substantially lifted. Manwaring's own designs, as illustrated in the 1765 *The Cabinet and Chair Makers' Real Friend and Companion,* tended to be much

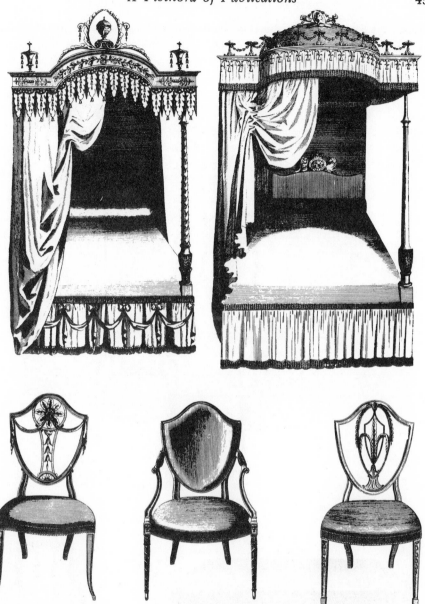

Excerpts from Hepplewhite's Guide

simpler than those of earlier designers, perhaps indicating that they were directed to a less-elevated clientele.

A minor landmark in pattern books was Matthias Lock's *New Book of Foliage for the Instruction of Young Artists* (1769). In it were featured for the first time engraved designs of furniture in the Adam manner, almost a decade after the turn to neoclassicism had begun.

Excerpts from Sheraton's Drawing Book

A much simplified neoclassicism was evident in the 1788 *The Cabinet Maker and Upholsterer's Guide* by George Hepplewhite, a work published after Hepplewhite's death by his widow. As almost nothing is known of Hepplewhite's cabinetwork, his reputation rests solely on the *Guide,* which shows the later French influence, especially in his chairs with their slightly carved, curved backs. The furniture designs shown in the *Guide* were not of Hepplewhite's own invention, but reflected existing modes. The *Guide's* furniture had a fragile appearance, but in reality it was quite strong and represented a structural advance from Chippendale's.

Like Hepplewhite, Thomas Sheraton is known much more for his designs than for the furniture that he produced in his over twenty

years of cabinetmaking. He was brought up a practical cabinetmaker and worked as one until 1790. Whatever styles he worked with as a cabinetmaker, as a designer Sheraton preferred furniture influenced by the French styles of the Consulate and Empire periods. The designs in his *Drawing Book*, published 1791–1794, tend to be severe yet charming and to show inventive touches often lacking in published designs. Like Chippendale's *Director*, Sheraton's *Drawing Book* was the object of much interest in the trade and included many furniture craftsmen in its subscription lists.

These pattern books and the many others published during the century shared certain features. They were all meant to enhance the reputations of their authors. Each of them emphasized the newness and novelty of the designs it contained. Their title pages liked to point out the fineness of their engraving and the usefulness they afforded workmen and would-be purchasers of good furniture. The practicality, elegance, and good taste of their contents were likewise self-proclaimed.

If we leniently concede the truth of these assertions, just how important were the pattern books published in eighteenth-century England?

From this distance in time it is difficult to say with any great precision. We cannot know, for example, how many cabinetmaking firms were moved to hire Thomas Johnson because of his publications or to what extent taste was improved because of William Chambers's attempt to purify the Chinese craze.

The best proof that we have of the success of the pattern books lies in their continuing publication. Someone obviously thought that they were worthwhile. Interest was widespread enough to enable assembly of impressive lists of subscribers for several of the books. People bought them, and the designers and cabinetmakers themselves thought the books worth the effort and initial expense of production. Some of the pattern books went through several editions, and many editions had more than one printing. There was at least one London business-man—Robert Sayer, a Fleet Street print-seller—who specialized in their sale.

The primary contemporary influence exercised by the trade catalogues was their dissemination of styles. In them, prospective purchasers of furniture could study a wide variety of available designs. Customers who found a visit to London inconvenient could use them as a guide for ordering furniture by mail or by messenger.

As the designs usually reflected rather than initiated fashion, the books were probably most useful to provincial cabinetmakers and to lesser London makers who did not employ a designer. The more-fashionable and larger London makers had their own designers who, at most, would have received inspiration from another designer's production. Any further recognition would have seemed an acknowledgment of the superiority of a competitor.

Exact copying of designs must have been unusual, for "book pieces," that is, articles of furniture matching a published design, are rare. When book pieces are found, they are usually simplified or modified.

In spite of the lack of data on the point, it seems sensible to assume that cabinetmakers and designers who published their ideas were generally more influential than those craftsmen who did not. Lacking design publication, the work of craftsmen exercised their creative influence only through the finished product, through the movement of workmen from one firm to another, and through apprentices who continued to work in the same style as their master after going into business for themselves.

For the modern student and collector, the furniture pattern books provide fascinating emphasis on the variety of eighteenth-century English furniture. More important, the publications demonstrate the ideal that the designers strove for: the designs that they would like to work with, as well as those that they had actually produced. In the pages of the best design books, practical limitations of material, finances, and craftsmanship were not overriding concerns. By studying these books we can more accurately assess what R. W. Symonds has called the "real value" of any era's furniture: "the aesthetic quality of its design."

4

From Walnutt-Tree to Satinwood

For many years, it was customary to classify eighteenth-century English furniture as being of the Age of Walnut or the Age of Mahogany, the dividing line between the two falling anywhere from the 1720s to the 1740s. As is the case with most convenient labels, these terms can be misleading.

There was an Age of Walnut and an Age of Mahogany only in that during certain periods of the century the very best English furniture tended to be made of one or the other of the woods. Even this recognition must be tempered with the knowledge that there was considerable overlapping of the two periods and that many woods other than walnut or mahogany were used in the construction of fine furniture.

Such encompassing labels have tended to slight the role played by materials other than wood. Upholstery, cane, marble, metal, and glass were used effectively by cabinetmakers of the period to make furniture more comfortable, useful, or ornamental.

The walnut-mahogany labels have also overshadowed the importance of how the wood was treated, yet during this century it was often the finish that gave furniture its distinctiveness. In several important styles, wood itself was little more than a well-shaped base for gilding, japanning, inlay, or painting.

Walnut was the most-popular furniture wood of the Restoration,

50

late Stuart, and early Georgian periods. Used during the Restoration
(after 1660) in its solid form, walnut soon became popular for veneer
and marquetry work because of its ornamental figure. Cabinetmakers
liked to use walnut in veneers because it meant that choice grains
could be used to decorate many more pieces of furniture. During the
reign of Queen Anne (1702–1714), walnut veneer came more and
more into use as the fashion continued for large, uncarved surfaces
in furniture.

There were three main types of veneer: the burr, the oyster-shell,
and the straight-cut. The burr was cut across the root of the tree,
giving a more finely marked figure and a mottled appearance. The
oyster-shell was cut transversely at an oblique angle from the smaller
branches of the tree, producing an oval figure. The straight-cut was
simply sliced lengthways from the trunk of the tree.

Although the beauty of walnut's veneers justified its popularity,
the wood had several disadvantages. Its conversion for use in furniture
necessitated much waste because the wood usually had many defects
and knots. The trunk of the walnut tree was not large enough to
make possible the construction of solid walnut tabletops, and the
wood's cost made impractical the carving of thick cabriole legs from
a single block of wood. The wood could not be easily carved. Most
disadvantageous, walnut was particularly susceptible to worms. Worms
literally proved the downfall of walnut as a fashionable furniture
wood, and we know that much walnut furniture of this period has
not survived because of the wood's susceptibility.

The walnut that we have been discussing was of English or Continental origin and was the wood in which much of the fine furniture
of Queen Anne's reign was made. The British colony of Virginia in
North America exported a variety of walnut that did not share these
defects.

Virginia or black walnut had been imported into England since
the early seventeenth century, but it was not until 1710–1720 that
English cabinetmakers began using it in any amount. In 1721 Parliament abolished the import duty on the colonial walnut, and its use
increased even more. Virginia walnut proved to be a very good furniture wood.

It had a good grain, a color—when freshly cut—like ebony, and a
high resistance to worms. Unlike its more ornamental predecessor, it
was free from knots and defects. It was also a large tree which could
be converted into large planks. Its log size enabled cabinetmakers to
use it for solid table tops and to carve from it bolder and more-massive

Queen Anne small bureau cabinet in black and bronze japanning, with mirror door; interior fitted with numerous small drawers and a cupboard; shelves and interior of bureau in scarlet lacquer, ca. 1710. Height: 5′4½″; Width: 1′9½″; Depth: 1′2¾″.

cabriole legs in one piece. A design by-product of Virginia walnut was the development of the tripod table, whose round top could be easily turned from a single slice of wood.

For all its virtues, Virginia walnut was not as attractive a wood as the earlier walnut varieties. It lacked the interesting grain, and for that reason was used mostly in solid form and not as a veneer.

Never as fashionable as either the earlier walnut had been or as mahogany soon became, Virginia walnut was nonetheless the wood from which many excellent chairs, tables, and chests were constructed. It is ironic that some articles of high-quality furniture from the reigns of George I (1714–1727) and George II (1727–1760) long thought to be mahogany were finally recognized as Virginia walnut. The humble

American walnut has aged so that it closely resembles faded mahogany, making identification of the woods difficult.

The old idea of an Age of Walnut and an Age of Mahogany has died hard. It is true that most top-quality furniture made in England between 1700 and 1730 was made of walnut and that mahogany then became the wood in which most fashionable cabinetmakers worked. It is equally true that some exceptional pieces of mahogany furniture were made as early as 1715 and that some very good cabinetmakers continued to work in walnut for decades after the Age of Walnut supposedly ended.

It is possible to quibble about the exact date on which mahogany assumed ascendancy. It is not possible to deny the enormous influence exerted by the wood. Mahogany had a decisive if not immediate impact upon the furniture world of eighteenth-century England. Its ac-

George I cabinet on stand in walnut veneer on oak with crossbanding in ash, ca. 1715.

ceptance can be traced in the importation statistics for the wood. In 1722, the year after the British government abolished the duty on its import, the total value of mahogany coming into England was £277, a figure which had risen to £6,430 by 1737 and to £30,000 in 1750.

The three most-important varieties of mahogany imported into England for furniture manufacture were Jamaican, Cuban, and Honduran. Jamaican, the variety imported until the 1740s, had very little figure and was therefore used mostly for solid work, not veneers. Cuban, appearing in the 1740s, had a very fine figure and was suitable for veneer work, but was expensive. The most-used mahogany after 1750 was the variety which came from Honduras, which was much lighter in color than the other varieties and which had a good-enough figure to allow for its being used in veneers.

All these mahoganies shared the wood's fortunate characteristics. It is, as R. W. Symonds has pointed out, the ideal furniture wood. The mahogany tree has little sap wood and suffers comparatively small shrinkage. The wood's straight, close grain makes it good for joinery work and for carving. It was obtainable during the eighteenth century in logs of large scantling; some mahogany trees measured as much as twelve feet in diameter. Mahogany's rich red color eventually fades to nut brown, both shades being attractive. Its finish acquires a polish easily. It is a very strong wood and very durable, for—most important—mahogany is worm free.

Mahogany's replacement of walnut as the most fashionable furniture wood was gradual; from 1725 to 1750 similar high-quality pieces could be had in either wood. As late as 1728, the successful cabinetmaker Daniel Bell lost over £500 in "walnut-tree plank" alone in the fire which destroyed his premises on St. Martin's Lane.

In 1732, when the auctioneer Surnam liquidated the stock of Thomas Tennant, the wholesale furniture dealer, his inventory threw an interesting light on the relative usage of mahogany and walnut at the time. As Surnam advertised in the London Daily *Post,* Tennant's stock included many pieces in walnut, some in mahogany alone, and several in both woods. Chimney glasses, chests upon chests, writing desks, and card tables could be had in walnut. Clothes chests and dining tables of all sizes were mahogany, while large desks, bookcases, "buroe" dressing tables, and chairs—"fine and coarse"—could be had in either wood.

A similar mixture of the two woods had been shown in Surnam's advertisement regarding the disposal of cabinetmaker James Faucon's furniture in 1731–1732. The "noted" Mr. Faucon's "fine works" seemed to include more articles made in both woods and a wider variety made in mahogany, perhaps reflecting the fact that the stock of an actual cabinetmaker might be more up to date than that of a furniture dealer.

Generally speaking, during these years most furniture to be carved was made from mahogany, and most uncarved pieces were made in the more ornamental walnut. This did not keep many cabinetmakers from using mahogany to construct the same designs that they had earlier executed only in walnut. In spite of the lack of good configuration in the early variety of mahogany, some cabinetmakers used it much as they had the more attractively marked walnut. Because of this continuing use of older designs, much of the earliest mahogany furniture is very plain without carved decoration.

It was, in fact, not until the close of the reign of George I that cabinetmakers began utilizing mahogany's unusual plasticity by indulging in more carved detail, especially upon chairs. At first, this carving incorporated only traditional motifs such as the lion and satyr mask, the shell and pendant, or the eagle head; and such decorative detail greatly enlivened the rather dull surface of Jamaican mahogany. As George II's reign progressed and cabinetmakers became more familiar with mahogany's capacity for carving, the basic shape of furniture began to show more variety and the carving became more elaborate and more integral a part of the construction. Much stylish furniture became curved, with serpentine, bow, or hollowed shapes. The legs of chairs, couches, and tables tended to become more substantial and to terminate with robust representations of ball-and-claw feet or hooves. The backs of chairs and settees abandoned their solid form, evolving into a pierced splat that allowed a carver ample opportunity to show his mechanical skill and inventiveness. The earlier decorative motifs remained popular, and were joined by Indian head and human female masks.

Another interesting development was the appearance of architectural features such as pediments, classical entablatures, and pilasters upon bureaus and bookcases. Moldings of case pieces, which had been cross-banded in walnut furniture, were enriched with carving.

At the mid-century, carvers and cabinetmakers put mahogany to a true test of its plasticity and strength as the wood was subjected to the intricacies necessitated by the newly popular rococo, Gothic, and Chinese styles.

Chairs were the first articles of furniture to sport the new styles. The top rail of their backs became serpentine, and the back splats

George I table in gesso, small size, ca. 1715.

showed the typical C- and S-shaped scroll curves of rococo. Their legs
often remained cabriole; but the curve of the leg was gentler and the
substantial ball-and-claw and heavy pad foot gave way to a lively
scroll. The straight-legged chair, complete with structurally unneces-
sary stretchers, reappeared after its fifty-year exile from fashion.

By the time that Chippendale first published his *Director* in 1754
the rococo, Chinese, and Gothic styles were so well established that
there were few pages of the pattern book that did not reveal their
influence. Even in the revised third edition of 1762, the same influences, somewhat toned down, were dominant. Mahogany was the ideal
wood for these complicated styles, and much rococo furniture was
made in mahogany. The carver's achievement was limited only by his
ability. He had a wood that would withstand almost any punishment
and clients eager to pay good prices for unusual work.

The introduction of the finely marked Cuban mahogany in the
1740s had brought about a return to some veneered furniture styles.
Patrons who demanded fashion at any cost had ordered furniture
featuring Cuban mahogany veneers as early as 1740. The most-expensive cabinetmakers, craftsmen like William Vile and Thomas Chip-

pendale, were known for their expert use of the new mahogany veneer.

As was to be expected from an age that demanded novelty, the exuberance of rococo ran its course, as had earlier styles. The catalytic agent of change was a young Scottish architect named Robert Adam, who had spent years in Italy absorbing what he considered the true spirit of the classical style. Upon his return to England in the late 1750s, he began at once translating this spirit into the form of elegant, lightly scaled, and colorful mansions.

George II chair of carved and gilded walnut with acanthus leaf decoration in gilt-pewter on the knees, ca. 1725–1750.

The kind of furniture envisioned by Adam and quickly adapted by leading furniture designers and craftsmen was, like his houses, much lighter in scale and more highly decorated than what had preceded it. The decoration took the form not of the elaborate carving that had gone before, but of exquisite inlay and of gilding and painted designs.

Mahogany was as suitable for this sort of work as it had been for the earlier styles, and it showed particularly to advantage in the simplified neoclassical styles of architect Henry Holland and of cabinetmaker-designer George Hepplewhite. The more severe, heavily French-inspired designs featured in Sheraton's *Drawing Book* (1790) did not demand so much of the wood and brought into vogue other woods, but mahogany remained the most-popular wood for fine furniture until the close of the eighteenth century.

Although walnut and mahogany must be allowed their joint ascendancy in the annals of eighteenth-century English furniture, there were other woods important to the manufacture of fine furniture.

There were the woods used for the carcases of the furniture to be covered with veneers. In the very finest and costliest furniture, oak was used for this purpose through much of the century; but in most furniture, deal was the most common carcase wood. Norway spruces and silver firs, planted long before in England, were the source for domestic deal. Imported deal came in the first half of the century from the Baltic and in the latter half from North America. The Baltic deal was known as the yellow, and the American as the red.

Then there were the relatively soft woods that were used for small, highly carved articles of furniture like mirrors and frames and console tables. Limewood was a popular wood for this use because it carved easily and took an exceptionally sharp outline.

Furniture that was to be painted or gilded did not require the fine figure of walnut or mahogany. Much furniture that was to be so treated was made in other, usually less-expensive domestic woods like beech, birch, elm, ash, fruitwoods, yew, chestnut, acacia, willow, and sycamore. Some of these cheaper woods could be stained so that they resembled and could be substituted for exotic but costly imported woods, for example: birch and chestnut for satinwood, acacia for tulipwood, stained pear and willow for ebony. Stained sycamore, known as silver-wood or harewood, was attractive and often used as a veneer in later eighteenth-century work.

Apart from mahogany, other imported and exotic cabinet woods that were important for furniture manufacture included padouk wood after 1725 and, in the last quarter of the century, rosewood and satinwood.

Since so much of the furniture of the century incorporated inlay or marquetry work, the exotic woods used for these purposes became important to cabinetmakers. Looking through pages of illustrations of eighteenth-century furniture, one can see satinwood inlaid with harewood and boxwood, padouk wood decorated with ebony and ivory, mahogany inlaid with tulipwood, satinwood inlaid with partridge wood, mahogany inlaid with kingwood, mahogany inlaid with satinwood, satinwood inlaid with rosewood, mahogany inlaid with fruitwoods—the combinations were endless. Other woods frequently used for decorative spot veneers and for bandings included fustic from the West Indies, Calamander from Ceylon, Coromandel from India, and thuya from Africa.

Wood, whether the humble variety or the more-exotic imported species, was the basic ingredient for almost all eighteenth-century English furniture, but there were other ingredients that played roles of varying importance. Textiles, cane, marble, glass, and metal were skillfully used by cabinetmakers.

Textiles were consistently the most-important secondary element. Upholstery was part of many articles of furniture throughout the century. The seats and often the backs of chairs, settees, and sofas were upholstered. Stool seats were upholstered. Firescreens framed textiles, and textiles were mounted upon sconces. Its voluminous

George III bureau bookcase in padouk wood with ebony and ivory detail, showing Anglo-Indian influence, ca. 1760. Height: 7'6"; Width: 3'7"; Depth: 2'.

hangings were often the most prominent and decorative part of a bed. The materials used for these purposes changed greatly from the beginning to the end of the century, not so much in actual fiber content as in color and design.

Leather, velvet, damask, silk, brocade, watered silk, watered woolen, tapestry, and tapestrylike embroidery were the most fashionable upholstery fabrics in the reigns of Queen Anne and the first two Georges. The colors of the fabrics were usually of the brilliant, primary school, for the late Stuarts and early Georgians were especially fond of vibrant color harmonies. The patterns of the fabrics were relatively unambitious and tended to be heavy, even clumsy in appearance in spite of the occasional enlivening foreign or exotic influence. The most

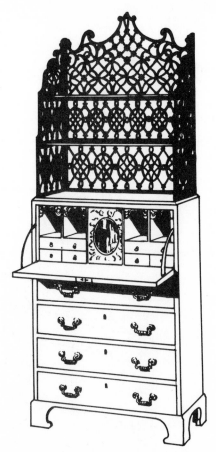

George III secrétaire cabinet in mahogany with finely carved open fretwork bookshelves, in the manner of Chippendale, ca. 1765. Height: 6'1"; Width: 2'4"; Depth: 1'1".

typical and successful fabric pattern of the period was flowers—singly, in bunches, strewn about, formally arranged, naturalistic, stylized. An especially popular upholstery for expensive furniture during the reigns of the first two Georges was Genoa velvet, a velvet with an overscaled pattern of conventionalized, overripe plant forms generally executed in deep red or green on a cream ground.

One of the most-appealing and widely used upholstery fabrics was embroidery. From the time of Queen Anne to the last decade of the reign of George II, embroidery was used for insertion into firescreens, for mounting upon sconces, for inlaying of card table tops, for covering stools, chairs, and settees. The most-favored stitches were gros point and petit point, which produced a tapestrylike surface.

Part of the appeal of embroidery lay in the fact that its patterns were limited only by the ability and interests of the embroiderer, and embroidery showed a much wider range in subject matter than other upholstery fabrics of the time. Flowers, birds, animals, fables, mythological scenes, country landscapes, people, exotic subjects—the list was long. One talented amateur needlewoman covered a set of chairs with a series of incidents taken from her family's history.

Most of this embroidery work was done by amateur needlewomen, and this was considered a suitable as well as a useful hobby for gentlewomen. Many of these women achieved a high level of competence, but few of them attempted to draw their own designs. Sometimes they turned to the village schoolmaster, who usually had at least the rudiments of an artistic education and who was glad to earn a few extra pence; sometimes they sought out a professional designer who would draw for them whatever they desired for their needle to trace. In addition, there were professional designers in London who turned out predrawn canvases to be sold to anyone whose fancy they caught, rather in the manner of today's needlework kits but with—one suspects— more evidence of skill in composition. These professional designers probably drew upon published works of engravings of flowers, animals, and historical events for their inspiration.

The kind of embroidery known as crewelwork, colored wool on white linen, was a popular holdover from Stuart times for bedhangings. Bedhangings enjoyed an importance that is difficult for us to realize today. From strictly functional drapery about a bed meant to keep away drafts and keep in warmth, bedhangings had evolved into a magnificent decorative device that only incidentally kept the drafts at bay. The finest fabrics were employed for this use. Crewel, silk embroidery, silk damasks, and the richest velvets were not too good for the decoration of the bed. Sometimes the bedhangings were so grand that they might be the single most-expensive item in an elegantly furnished house. Hundreds of yards of costly material were required for the ample effect so desired, and just the trim for this much material could be worth many times the value of the bed itself. The William Kent-designed state bed at Houghton, for example, was outfitted with its green velvet draperies in 1732, and the cost of the gold braid and embroidery trim alone amounted to over £1,200.

Tapestry remained a popular upholstery fabric for chairs, settees, and screens although English efforts to establish domestic tapestry production facilities were only partially successful. The tapestry designs used for upholstery were of vases, flowers, scroll work, animals, birds, and naturalistic blossoms.

During the last decade of the reign of George II and until the end of the century, upholstery became much less flamboyant than it had been earlier. Some of the same fabrics remained favorites. Leather was still important, as was velvet, but in plain muted shades not in the brilliant colors of yesteryear. Soft-toned watered silks and silk mixtures were widely used. Damask tended to be one color on white. Pale brocaded satins and light-colored plain satins went well with the new furniture styles. The most-popular fabric for chairs and settees was striped satin.

Embroidery of the gros and petit point variety was going out of style, and its use became increasingly rare after 1765 because it did not harmonize with the more-restrained interiors coming into vogue. When embroidery was used, it was ordinarily in the form of flat flowers or urns and other classical symbols on a pale satin ground; but more-prosaic designs, including maps, were also executed for upholstery. At one point, there was even a rage for embroidered pictures, done "after" some old or new master. These pictures—thankfully—were usually hung on the wall, not draped across the seat of a chair.

Embroidery's close relation, tapestry, was rarely used for upholstery after 1760 except *en suite* in a "tapestry room." These tapestry rooms were usually main reception rooms in some great house whose walls were hung with specially designed tapestry panels fitted to the room, which was furnished with several chairs, stools, and settees or couches covered in coordinated tapestry.

Painted and printed textiles became acceptable in the last quarter of the century, but they were rarely used on furniture of the best quality. Found extensively in less—grand settings, these humbler textiles were used for bedhangings and chair and settee upholstery. Silk

George II carved and giltwood pier glass, ca. 1750. Height: 6'8"; Width: 4'.
George III carved and giltwood side table with marble top; attributed to
Samuel Norman, after a design by Robert Adam, ca. 1770.

and cotton were the fabrics most often used for painted textiles, and
the English versions took their cue from the floral patterns on a white
satin ground that had been imported from China.

Early in the century chairs and settees that were not upholstered
sometimes had cane seats and backs. The fashion for cane was originally imported into Europe from the Portuguese settlements in the
East Indies and from Goa in India about the middle of the seventeenth
century. The Dutch, the Portuguese, and the English made much use

of cane in the years following its introduction. Cane, produced from the fronds of the palms of the Calamus family, was erroneously termed rattan when it was imported from the East Indies by the East India Company.

Cane chairs were so popular in England in the last quarter of the seventeenth century that a separate trade—the cane–chair maker—emerged, and this new kind of craftsman competed keenly with the makers of other sorts of chairs. When cane chairs went out of favor during the reign of George I, the cane-chair makers began to turn to the manufacture of other sorts of chairs, encroaching on the regular chair trade of the joiners and upholsterers.

A trade card probably typical of the cane-chair makers during this difficult transitional period was that of William Old and John Ody, "at the Castle in St. Paul's Church-Yard, over-against the South–Gate of ye Church, London." Old and Ody, both members of the Joiners Company in the 1720s, advertised that they made and sold "all sorts of Cane & Dutch Chairs, Chair Frames for Stuffing and Cane-Sashes. And also all sorts of the best Looking-Glas & Cabinet-Work in Japan, Walnut-Tree & Wainscot, at reasonable Rates."

Cane was revived at least temporarily in Chippendale's *Director* when he suggested that a series of chairs in the Chinese manner commonly had cane bottoms with loose cushions.

Like cane, metal played a sporadically important role. Gerrit Jensen, probably the most-fashionable cabinetmaker in London between 1689 and 1715, employed an unusual metal marquetry in his work. John Channon, who worked in London from the mid-1730s until well past the mid-century, made in the 1740s some furniture that featured engraved brass-inlay and that was mounted in ormolu, a cast and gilt brass. In some styles, brass studs were used to trim chair upholstery. Ormolu, usually in the form of gilt bronze or brass, was most popular for handles, while chased brass was often used for glazing bars. In connection with the use of metal fittings should be mentioned the introduction, during this century, of screws to be used in place of nails to secure such fittings to wood.

Marble, on the other hand, was used throughout much of the century, as a solid slab and in inlaid form. From the early Georgian period when the ornately carved and gilt side tables inspired by William Kent were almost invariably topped by marble slabs or marble mixtures until the marble-topped giltwood side tables of Adam's time, marble was rarely out of fashion. Rather, its use was generally confined to certain types of furniture. Side tables, some console table tops, columns and the like were often marble no matter how ornate or how refined the base that supported them. The marble, most of it imported from Italy, could be almost any color—green, pink, gold, even white. Marble tops were specially popular for pier tables, tables that stood beneath large mirrors between the sizable windows of the century. So common was the use of marble for sideboards that Chippendale felt constrained to point out in his third edition of the *Director* that a particular sideboard should be made with a wooden top, as the base was "too slight for Marble-Tops." Cabinetmakers were apparently always ready to supply these marble-topped tables, and furniture shops stocked a variety of them.

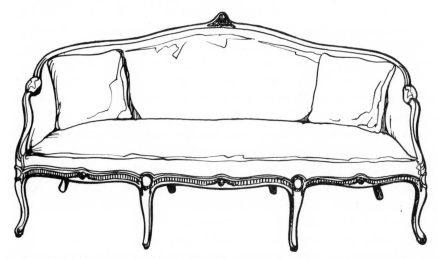

George III painted settee in the French taste, with blue and apricot decoration on an ivory ground, ca. 1780. Height: 35½"; Width: 6'1"; Depth: 2'.

Sometimes, scagliola was used as a substitute for solid marble. Scagliola contained marble in the form of small chips that were imbedded in a composition of plaster of Paris and glue. The composition was then colored to taste and polished.

The use of glass, both clear and in the form of mirrors, not only continued throughout the century; it actually increased due to improvements in the domestic glass industry. A near-monopoly situation had enabled English glassmakers to fall far behind Continental glassmakers as the century progressed, primarily in the area of the large glass needed for the oversized mirrors becoming so popular; but in the 1770s a consortium was formed to establish an English glassmaking concern that would employ the most-advanced glassmaking techniques, making possible the English production of the large looking glasses. Until that time English cabinetmakers wishing to employ the large glasses had to order them from abroad, usually from Paris, and the cost of importing these large plates of glass was very high because of the freight and insurance charges.

Glass remained relatively expensive during the century, as was seen in the continuing practice of many cabinetmakers and other craftsmen to advertise that they would "new polish" old glasses and reframe them in a new fashion. Even so, English cabinetmakers made ample use of glass.

The most-obvious use for glass, of course, was in mirrors. The English glassmakers produced an excellent looking glass, though limited in size, from the early years of the century. The improved quality of domestic looking glass resulted in the increased popularity of mirrors.

People of fashion had stopped thinking of looking glasses as precious luxuries, and had begun viewing them as part of the furniture of a room. As a result, looking-glass frames tended to reflect furniture styles. Such frames were made from a popular cabinet wood such as walnut or were carved from a soft wood like limewood, then gilded. Apart from mirrors as such, looking glass was also used to front sconces, thus giving extra value to the reflected candlelight.

Until 1720 the trade of the looking-glass maker was usually distinct, but after that date it often ceased to be a separate craft and became part of the trade in cabinetmaking and upholstering. This development reflected the increasing importance of glass in furniture, especially in the doors of bookcases and cupboards.

Fashion, which often dictated the use of a certain wood or of a specific kind of textile, was just as influential in the choice of the finish that was to be applied to the article of furniture when it was carved and assembled. Japanning, gilding, gesso, inlay, and decorative painting were finishes popular at one point or another during the century.

One of the more-colorful holdovers from the seventeenth-century into the reign of Queen Anne was japanned furniture. The East India Company, a British corporation dating from 1600, had a monopoly on trade with the Eastern Hemisphere. The Company had found during the seventeenth century that there was an active market in England for the products of a part of the world still viewed by many Englishmen as a mysterious "never-never land."

The countries of the East, primarily India and China, produced some articles which the Company could and did import, but Eastern

needs and tastes did not always parallel those of England. Acting with
the ingenuity that seems common to big business in any century, the
East India Company had solved this problem in the early 1670s by
sending English craftsmen to India equipped with English patterns
for an assortment of merchandise, their aim to teach Indian workmen
how to make goods that would find a ready market in England and
Europe.

One branch of endeavor covered by this interesting early example
of cooperative economic development was furniture manufacture.
Guided by the teachings of their English instructors, the Indians were
soon exporting japanned furniture specifically designed to appeal to
English taste. Constructing bodies of chairs, tables, chests, and bureaus
in traditional English forms, the foreign workmen then applied a
tough lacquer finish which was decorated with various exotic motifs.
A brisk trade soon developed in such goods, not only from India but
also from China.

So successful, in fact, was the trade in japanned and other furniture
that concerned parties in England began to protest the export of gold
bullion to meet its cost. One suspects that the concerned parties might
have been English cabinetmakers who did not like such aggressive

George III painted armchair, in the manner of Hepplewhite, ca. 1785.

foreign competition, for in 1700 the Joiners' Company petitioned
Parliament to restrict the free importation of furniture from the East
Indies. The joiners claimed that the imports were injuring the business
of English craftsmen. In 1710 the domestic japanners followed the example of the joiners, and petitioned the government to suppress the
import of "Indian lacquer."

Although English craftsmen may not have liked the competition
posed by the imports, they were quick to sense the sale appeal of
japanned furniture. The English workmen had some advantages over
their oriental and Indian counterparts. What English lacquer lacked
in quality—it was not nearly so tough or smooth as the oriental
lacquer—it gained in appeal. The limited color and decorative range
of oriental lacquer compared unfavorably with the wide assortment
of color and decoration available on English japanned furniture.

Perhaps the most-attractive examples of English japanned furniture
were the lighthearted secrétaires and chests with their bright finish,
often a striking red or green, gaily decorated with the English workman's somewhat whimsical idea of oriental motifs. The carcases for
japanned furniture were usually deal, beech, lime, or pearwood. Master japanners probably bought these carcases from cabinetmakers, then
japanned and sold them. The japanning itself consisted only of a
transparent varnish over a type of oil painting.

From tradesmen's cards still in existence, it is clear that there were
a sizable number of London craftsmen who specialized in or who felt
themselves competent to produce japanned furniture in the early
eighteenth century. Japanned furniture remained fashionable until the
1720s, then declined in popularity until its reappearance with the advent of the Chinese Chippendale style of the 1750s and early 1760s.
In their pattern books, both Chippendale and Ince & Mayhew featured
designs in this style meant for japanning. In the third edition of the
Director, Chippendale suggested that an extremely elaborate china
case, a highly detailed china shelf, two ornate ladies' dressing tables,
and some rococo stands for china jars would look well japanned. Ince
& Mayhew showed in *Universal System* two china cases and two
candlestands, very much in the current Chinese taste, meant to be
japanned.

Although Indian and Chinese japanned goods, the original inspiration for English japanned furniture, were subjected to import restrictions, which reduced their flow into England, they had been the
forerunner of a picturesque style that offered a spicy accent whenever
it was in vogue.

Another bright accent was provided by gesso furniture. Gesso was a type of furniture in which the plain wood carcase—usually deal, beech, limewood, or pearwood—of a piece of furniture was covered by many coats of whiting which formed a gesso ground in which a highly skilled workman carved low-relief decorative ornament. High-relief motifs on a gesso piece were first carved in wood, then finished in gesso. The background of the carving was often punched with a circular stamp to circumvent the difficulty of obtaining a smooth, level finish on the uncarved gesso ground, a technique that also served to highlight the carved portions by providing a matte effect background. The whole piece was then covered with gold or, more rarely, silver.

Originally introduced from the Continent, gesso was quickly appreciated by the wealthy, who liked its elegance and spontaneity and also the fact that its high cost kept it relatively exclusive. The best gesso pieces possessed a pleasing airiness and individuality quite different from wood carving.

Gesso was especially favored for more-ornamental and decorative furniture, such as pier tables, looking-glass frames, stands of various kinds, sconces, chandeliers, and fire screens. It was also used, however, for large chests on stands and even for whole suites of furniture, including chairs, stools, and couches. Sometimes, suites of walnut furniture would be decorated with panels of gesso work and gesso moldings.

James Moore, partner of the progressive and aggressive John Gumley of Glass-House fame, was particularly well known in the first quarter of the century for his fine gesso work, whose carving was clearly inspired—as was most gesso carving—by French ornamental designs then being published in England. The Crown ordered several pieces of Moore's fine furniture between 1716 and 1726 for various Royal Palaces.

The basic disadvantage of gesso was its relative fragility, a quality which meant that in spite of its thirty years or so of popularity at the beginning of the century, not many examples remain today.

Gesso furniture was not the only kind of furniture meant to be gilded. Another import from France, gilt furniture, remained stylish through much of the century in one form or another. Gilt was consistently acceptable as the finish for pier tables, for the elaborately carved supports provided for large marble slabs, and for picture- and looking-glass frames. By mid-century it was coming into more-general use. Pattern books of the time show that dressing tables, candlestands, stands for jars, fire screens, table frames, important beds, back-stool chairs, candlesticks, and pier-glass frames were meant sometimes to be finished in gilt. Later in the century, gilt remained popular for frames, fire screens, and console and side tables, and was also used sometimes to finish the exposed wood portions of elegant chairs in the French taste.

George III mahogany arm chair, the back carved with a spray of flowers and foliage, in the manner of Hepplewhite, ca. 1790.

Painted furniture became stylish only very late in the century, and the painted design was usually meant to complement inlay work. Furniture to be painted was ordinarily of some less-expensive wood since its grain was not important. The finished piece was given several good coats of paint, then decorated with the painted design.

Wood furniture that was not to be painted or gilded or lacquered was usually finished with either a variety of oil or polished with wax. Sometimes the most-expensive furniture was treated with a polished varnish, a time-consuming process.

Inlaid furniture, as was pointed out earlier, was usually of one wood, such as walnut or mahogany or satinwood, inlaid with either a design or banding in a contrasting wood veneer or sometimes even metal. The inlaid design was actually set into the surface of the cabinet body wood. Inlay was one of the most-attractive features of much furniture of the reigns of Queen Anne and George III. When referred to as marquetry, inlay was a more-intricate technique in which different kinds, colors, and textures of woods were cut and fitted together to create a pattern—a picture or design in wood. Marquetry was popular during the very early years of Queen Anne's reign in the Dutch-inspired furniture of the time, and came back into favor with the neoclassical furniture inspired by Adam. Marquetry became so popular during the neoclassical period that some marquetry workers set themselves up as specialists and supplied the trade at large from their own premises.

Although it was undoubtedly beautiful, marquetry had its limitations. It was very difficult and expensive to produce and subject to decay. The remaining examples of eighteenth-century English marquetry show how well English craftsmen assimilated this idea from Holland. Some authorities feel that the inlaid neoclassical furniture was the most-outstanding body of work produced by English craftsmen during this century. Ralph Edwards and Margaret Jourdain, for example, feel that Chippendale's best work was of this genre, and was at least comparable to the greatest French marquetry of the period.

Cabinetmakers and other practicing furniture craftsmen needed materials with specific qualities to produce their work. At times the furniture craftsman's choice of materials was dictated by fashion or personal preference, and at times his choice of style and method of execution was greatly influenced by the materials available to him.

The eighteenth-century English furniture craftsman was fortunate in both the quality and quantity of the raw materials that were his for the ordering. England's ever-increasing international trade constantly enlarged the cabinetmaker's creative possibilities by bringing to his attention new woods, new finishes, and new techniques. The natural resources of much of the world and the best of other nations' goods could be his, and London was the chief importing center where all these useful, exotic, and often beautiful treasures ended their long ocean voyages. Woods of seemingly endless variety and with names redolent of wild and distant forests; elegant brocades and lush velvets reminiscent of the gaiety of their Italian origin; sumptuous damasks; even homely feathers—all this and much more appeared in London markets daily.

George III finely carved gilt mirror with pagoda top, in the manner of Chippendale, ca. 1760. Height: 5'8"; width: 3'9".

From the wide variety of materials available to him, the English craftsman rapidly learned which were most suitable for a particular use, and applied this knowledge so well that one of the outstanding characteristics of eighteenth-century English cabinetmaking is the way in which the material quite often is so complementary as to have become integral to the design. Undoubtedly there were failures, but more often the choice and treatment of the many ingredients were remarkably successful.

5
Wealth, Position, and Power

The style-setters who patronized the fashionable cabinetmakers and architects were people whose position and way of life required impressive surroundings and whose wealth gave them the means of obtaining whatever was necessary to ensure that their homes adequately conveyed just how high that position was and how vast the wealth that adorned it. In eighteenth-century England wealth, position, and power were not only complementary, but often interdependent.

There was a tangible reason for men of wealth to buy and improve property, for land possession carried with it political rights as well as social standing. The rich commercial class especially craved the privileges conferred by the land and rushed to buy it and to place upon it dwellings that would rival those of the noblemen.

In a way, a man's choice of surroundings was brick and stone, wood and velvet evidence of who and what he was. The house that he built, remodeled, or decorated could be an instantaneous and irrevocable revelation to his contemporaries of his politics, his ambitions, his education, his travels, his economic status, and—most important—his taste.

Taste was a commodity that obsessed upper-class Englishmen of the century. An import from Italy about 1615, the concept of taste as the recognition of positive, firm values set by a select company

73

was the one fixed and seemingly immutable concern of the 1700s. That taste was a nebulous, virtually indefinable term that was inherently relative and highly subjective did not keep many well-to-do Englishmen from devoting their efforts and fortunes to its service.

The preoccupation with taste was so extreme that it became the butt of much ridicule and satire in less-fashionable levels of life. A writer for *The Connoisseur* in 1756 sneered:

> Blest age! when all men may procure
> The title of a Connoisseur;
> When noble and ignoble herd
> Are govern'd by a single word.

Yet satires of "this amazing superabundancy of Taste" did not disturb the peers, politicians, and mere moneymakers whose more-intellectual representatives could point to the moral philosophy of Anthony Ashley-Cooper, third Earl of Shaftesbury, to justify the search for good taste. To his contemporaries and equals of the late seventeenth and early eighteenth centuries Shaftesbury seemed to be saying that good taste and moral superiority were dual and coeval. If a man were an inherently superior person, his superiority would reveal itself in his surroundings as well as in his behavior and beliefs. Since Shaftesbury's publications were not notable for their clarity or consistency, Georgians could interpret them much as they pleased; but it is doubtful that men of fashion would have denied the connection between taste and superiority, whether in the form of cause and effect or as two necessarily coexisting qualities. The concrete result of this general acceptance and interpretation of Shaftesbury's moral musings was that —as James Lees-Milne has pointed out—there was a growing tendency to believe that "correct breeding and correct architecture went hand in hand."

This belief, combined with the extraordinarily catholic interests of English gentlemen, had interesting consequences. For one thing, it led to architectural "posing" by aristocrats. Architectural design was a very chic thing with which to amuse oneself, and it proved that one was a person of taste and accomplishment. It was quite probable that some nobles were not above hiring designers, then claiming authorship credit for their designs. For another, the whole obsession with taste initiated an extremely stylish game in which the rich, powerful, and titled seemed to live only to view, judge, and comment—often quite volubly—upon the dwelling places of their kind. This was the generation that could understand and applaud Pope's couplet:

Know then thyself, presume not God to scan:
The proper study of mankind is Man.

Their way of life facilitated the "proper study" nicely, for all the "people worth knowing" were known to each other. They sat in boxes or, until the time of Garrick, actually on the stage itself and laughed together at the comedies of Vanbrugh, Congreve, Fahrquar, Cibber, Colman, and Goldsmith. They attended the same grand fetes at the court or the princely London houses belonging to their mutual cousins (almost everybody was everybody else's cousin at some remove). They journeyed to great country estates where they hunted, rode, and went to cockfights together. They gambled together at White's in London, talked politics together at the Rumpsteak. They had their portraits painted by the same fashionable artists. They passed along to one another or even shared their mistresses. They raced their horses over the same tracks. As youths they crisscrossed Europe in droves, constantly encountering one another, the same guidebooks in their luggage, the same sort of tutors by their sides.

They even found time to sit in Parliament together, some in Commons, more in Lords. They founded the forerunners of the learned societies together, and supported the establishment of the British Museum (1753) and the Royal Academy (1768).

In short, they sported, traveled, dallied, drank, and generally raised hell together; and when that palled or got the best of their overtaxed constitutions, they recuperated together. They drank the waters at Scarborough or Buxton or Bath, or perhaps Tunbridge, Cheltenham, or Spa. Wherever they went and whatever they did, they could be sure of finding their own kind, so circumscribed was the life that they led.

This insularity bred an understandable familiarity. It was not to be wondered that their favorite topic of contemplation and conversation was themselves. This was what they knew best, what concerned them most intimately. Hardly censorious in most matters, these people were firm upon the point of good taste. If a man possessed it, he would be forgiven much else. If he did not, his other merits, however great they might be, were publicly diminished.

As Lory says in Vanbrugh's *The Relapse,* "We seldom care for those that don't love what we love." Perhaps the preoccupation with taste had that simple an origin. People who want and who try to be fashionable themselves can rarely understand, much less forgive, those who do not.

This did not mean that even "people of taste" always agreed. It was quite possible for Edward Harley, second Earl of Oxford, to dismiss Sir Robert Walpole's Houghton Hall as being in poor taste, especially complaining of its "most monstrous" profusion of mahogany furnishings. Or for the Duke of Devonshire's magnificent Chatsworth to be described by John Byng, later fifth Viscount Torrington, as "this vile house" full of "uncomfortable rooms and frippery French furniture."

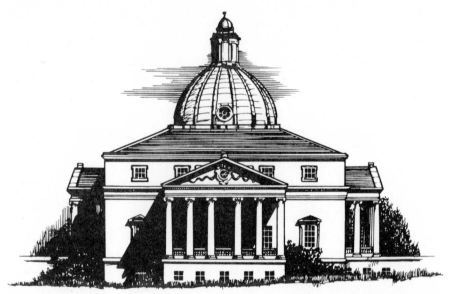

Mereworth Castle, Kent: *Designed for John Fane, later seventh Earl of Westmorland, in 1720–1723 by architect Colin Campbell, author of* Vitruvius Britannicus. *Adapted from Palladio's design for the Rotonda, or Villa Capra. Described by Nigel Nicolson as "a remarkable incident in the long flirtation between Italy and the Gothic North."*

What was fashionable, that is, what was considered to be in good taste, did not remain constant, and this lack of constancy was nowhere more noticeable than in architecture. What people of taste accepted unquestionably one decade, they might reject out of hand the next, thus Vanbrugh, Hawksmoor, Gibbs, Campbell, Burlington, Kent, Taylor, Stuart, Adam, Chambers, Holland, Wyatt, and Soane—architects who were successively fashionable during the century—could be de rigueur one year, passé the next.

Taste was even subdivided into kinds of taste that recognized certain social, economic, and political differences. One could speak of a house as in "humble taste" or "rich taste." It was possible for an aristocrat to speak of a house of the 1730s as very good, but in the old baroque taste, or for an adherent of Adam's in the 1760s to pass a similar judgment on the works of the Palladians.

Men often built or remodeled houses according to their political affiliations. From 1715 onwards, Palladianism was strongly identified with the newly powerful Whigs, who rarely planned a building project without at least consulting Richard Boyle, third Earl of Burlington, or one of his fellow Palladians. The rich, out-of-power, often Roman Catholic Tories reacted by continuing to patronize Wren-inspired architects like James Gibbs, himself a Tory and a Roman Catholic. Feelings sometimes ran high over these architectural schools, the Tories being particularly resentful of Colin Campbell, author of *Vitruvius Britannicus* in 1715 and a leader, along with Burlington and William Kent, of the Palladians. In wealthy, conservative country circles, the baroque style of Vanbrugh and Nicholas Hawksmoor continued to appear in new houses until the mid-century, as their builders were distrustful equally of the political and the architectural innovations of the London-based Whigs.

The political pendulum had swung the other way by 1768 when the astute Robert Adam thought it worth his while to sit in the House of Commons as a Tory member for Kinrossshire, a seat he held until relinquishing it in 1774. The closing decades of the century saw another swing as Henry Holland worked only for the inner circle of Great Whigs that surrounded the Prince of Wales, later Regent, then George IV.

A notable exception to the reasonably clear-cut distinctions established in architectural preference by politics and even religion was the successful poet Alexander Pope. Pope, a Tory and a Catholic and well established in the highest levels of Tory society, was extremely interested in the development of Palladianism in England although he could not resist taking occasional potshots at its undisciplined spread in the hands of "imitating fools."

He consulted Burlington, a close personal friend, before making improvements to his own house. Pope's extensive knowledge of the classics and his familiarity with Shaftesbury's moral philosophy made him an ideal arbiter of taste for his contemporaries, who listened to his opinions on architecture and gardening as avidly as they read his "scandalous" poetry. Perhaps Pope's most-influential work of this sort was his essay on landscape architecture which mercilessly ridiculed the early eighteenth-century taste for stiff, formal, unnatural gardens.

Pope's long association with Allan Bathurst, Earl of Bathurst, in planning and reworking Bathurst's extensive grounds illustrated the poet's genuine interest in this topic and his determination that Englishmen should abandon artificiality in favor of a more-natural approach.

Political and religious influences were woven into the tapestry of eighteenth-century architecture as a definite, but sometimes barely perceptible thread. The point at which the thread of influence was most prominent was from 1720 to 1750, when the ruling Whigs managed to translate their political philosophy of stability and order-from-chaos into the brick and stone of Palladianism so well that the architectural movement became forever linked with the so-called Whig Ideal.

If the Whig Ideal was the most-obvious manifestation of the interaction between political and artistic philosophies, it was nevertheless only one manifestation. Throughout the century the interrelationship remained strong. If Burlington's Chiswick epitomized the Whig Ideal in the 1720s, Adam's Kedleston Hall represented the Tory reaction of the 1760s.

The one strain of influence that permeated the bulk of English architecture and colored the work of most of the leading architects after 1720 was the classical. First it was the classical as interpreted by Palladio as reinterpreted by Burlington, then the archaeological classical of Robert Adam, and finally the even more academic classical of Henry Holland. The classical remained useful to architects because it was a basic style upon which their patrons had been presold.

The reasons for this were twofold: the education and the travels of the wealthy. Their education was almost wholly classical; this was learning that enhanced a gentleman's character without sullying his mind with academic trivia. Their travels, especially the Grand Tour, were usually an extension of this education, focusing as they did on Italy. As impressionable young men of wealth, therefore, they were exposed to the twin lures of that nation's appealing climate and people and its wealth of classical buildings and ruins. Upon their return home the more observant of the young travelers must have shared William Kent's opinion of "this Gothick country" of England.

All young men of wealth and breeding took the Grand Tour, usually accompanied by at least one tutor. The trip was supposed to provide the finishing touches to their education and to coat the young with a cultural veneer before their official entry into polite English society as adults.

If a young man were attentive and had a good tutor, the tour could fulfill the highest expectations of fond parents and guardians. Otherwise, it could be either an exercise in debauchery or an episode of acute homesickness and boredom.

When these well-traveled and classically educated gentlemen began to think of house building or remodeling, they could seek inspiration, if they chose, from the large number of architectural pattern books that were published during the century. In subject matter the publications ranged from the most-conservative Palladianism to murky Gothic to fantastic Chinese and were often published by subscription, the subscribers usually including many of the men who had the means and the position to justify building the most impressive of the books' designs.

Isaac Ware's 1738 edition of *The Four Books of Andrea Palladio's Architecture,* for example, included among its subscribers not only architects, architectural craftsmen, untitled men of wealth, and thirty lesser nobles, but also three Dukes and sixteen Earls. Publications like Ware's *Palladio* were, of course, basically reprints of earlier foreign works translated into English with perhaps some additional comments by the translator.

A second kind of architectural publication was the publishing by one English architect of a fellow architect's designs. William Kent's *The Designs of Inigo Jones* (1727) and John Vardy's *Some Designs of Mr. Inigo Jones and Mr. William Kent* (1744) were of this sort.

The third and most numerous category of publication included designs published and explained by their own architects. Usually the architects directed these books towards both professional builders and gentlemen interested in architecture. This aim was spelled out in the title of a monthly publication of the 1770s:

> The Builder's Magazine: or Monthly Companion for Architects, Carpenters, Masons, Bricklayers, etc., as well as for Every Gentlemen who would wish to be a competent Judge of the elegant and necessary Art of Building.

One suspects that *The Builder's Magazine,* which was supposed to make workmen "equally capable to erect a Cathedral, a Mansion, a Temple, or a Rural Cot," was a humbler successor to works like James Gibbs's *Book of Architecture* (1728), whose success earned its author £1,900, or Sir William Chambers's *A Treatise on the Decorative Part of Civil Architecture* (1759). All of these publications, however, afforded to the young man a means of improving his taste. He could

read them and be well equipped to be considered generally knowledge-
able on the subject of architecture by all but the most expert of his
peers.

The Vyne, Hampshire: *A product of the sixteenth, seventeenth, and eighteenth centuries, its interiors were redecorated by John Chute in the mid-
eighteenth century.*

That these usually expensive architectural books were well received
was proved by the stream of them that appeared during the century.
There were designers like Batty Langley and William Halfpenny who
made the production of such books an important part of their life-
work, so numerous were their publications, and rare was the architect
who did not publish his designs at some time.

So unending seemed the continuing stream of the books that even
one of the more-prolific architect-authors could not resist spoofing the
trend. In his own *Architecture Improved* (1755), Robert Morris in-
serted an ad for:

> A Treatise on Country Five Barr'd Gates, Stiles and Wickets, elegant Pig-
> styles, beautiful Henhouses, and delightful Cowcribs, superb Cart-houses,
> magnificent Barn Doors, variegated Barn Racks, and admirable Sheep-
> Folds; according to the Turkish and Persian manner. . . . To which is
> added, some Designs of Fly-traps, Bee Palaces, and Emmet Houses, in The
> Muscovite and Arabian architecture; all adapted to the Lattitude and
> Genius of England. The whole entirely new, and inimitably designed in
> Two Parts, on Forty Pewter Plates, under the immediate Inspection of
> Don Gulielmus De Demi Je ne sai Quoi, chief Architect to the Grand
> Signor.

It is impossible to ascertain the exact effect of any individual architectural publication although it is clear that books like Campbell's
Vitruvius Britannicus and the Leoni and Ware editions of *Palladio*
were influential; but as a group the publications must have had considerable influence on estate builders.

Another important influence was the aristocratic way of life. The well-placed Englishman's home had not only to reflect his status and taste, but also to house the activities of himself, his family and guests, as well as the servants needed to maintain such a liberal establishment. The typical upper-class Englishman of the century thought as little of entertaining large numbers of people for a week as for a weekend.

Because of the importance of public life, great houses tended to devote what seems a disproportionate amount of their space to large and magnificent suites of rooms meant only for entertaining. This need for impressiveness led, particularly in Palladian houses, to the practice of opening reception rooms out of one another. This practice did open up dramatic vistas (in some of the great houses, such as Holkham Hall, it is possible to stand in one doorway and see in a straight line for hundreds of feet across the interior of the entire building), but necessitated rooms in a square or rectangular shape boasting corresponding door positioning, an arrangement that must at times have posed problems of convenience. Although liberated to a degree from squares and rectangles, the architecture of Adam and his successors continued to reveal the emphasis placed on sumptuous reception rooms geared for elaborate and frequent entertaining. At no point in the century did convenience concern most house builders nearly as much as that the finished house reflect their good taste and openhandedness.

The effect of the whole estate—the right sort of house set in the right sort of grounds—did not obsess patrons to the exclusion of the house's interior. Important as the whole might be to reinforce an estate builder's good idea of himself, it was inside the house that his personal taste most forcefully showed itself. The concern with the house's interior—its wallcoverings, its rugs, its furniture, its objets d'art—was activated by Kent when he embraced the concept of each room in a house as an aesthetic entity, an individual creation which was important both in itself and as a part of the whole.

This was a fairly new development. As late as the reign of Queen Anne, even great houses were furnished in a relatively sparse manner. Their lofty rooms usually had wainscotted walls encompassing only a few pieces of utilitarian furniture. The master's bed was probably the single most-important and obviously expensive piece of furniture in the house.

With the advent of the Georgian era, furniture began to play a more-important role; and when Kent treated furniture as part of a house's interior architecture, the incentive and pressure to furnish

Kedleston, Derbyshire: *The product of three talented architects—Matthew Brettingham, Sr., James Paine, and Robert Adam—Kedleston Hall was built by Sir Nathaniel Curzon 1758–1770. The interior is almost entirely Adam's.*

houses more carefully increased. More attention was paid to wall-coverings, window hangings and the like, and it was a rare house builder of means who did not engage someone like decorator and paperhanger Thomas Bromwich to attend to such details.

Naturally, all this grandeur and elegance carried a price tag that put it out of the reach of most Englishmen. At a time when a modest house could be furnished for a few pounds, Chippendale could charge Sir Rowland Winn of Nostell Priory £72.10.0 for a library table. The prices of the best cabinetmakers seem quite reasonable by today's standards, even allowing for inflation and money revaluation, but we must remember that ready money was a fairly rare commodity at the time. Good cabinetmakers made less-costly items, it is true—Vile and Cobb made a "good wallnuttree buerow on casters" for Anthony Chute of the Vyne in 1752–53 for only £5.10.0—but the very best of their work bore a price tag that reflected the high quality of the materials and the craftsmanship that had gone into it.

The houses in which the furniture sat could cost large fortunes. Blenheim Palace, given the Duke of Marlborough by "a grateful nation" but partially paid for by Marlborough himself, cost over £200,000. The ninth Duke of Norfolk spent approximately £100,000 to build a 500-room house at Worksop and furnish it. When the house burned in 1761, less than a month after its completion, Norfolk immediately began another. Even improvements to existing structures could be costly. In the 1780s George John, second Earl Spencer, spent over £20,000 to alter his home.

In a time when a man of reasonable needs and wishes could live quite comfortably, freed from the necessity of toil, on an income of a few-hundred pounds a year, these figures were significant. It was obvious that there was an impressive concentration of wealth in the hands of a certain economic and social class. Peers, especially those holding long-established titles, had the jump on money accumulation because they often held large blocks of land throughout the country that were suitable for development or exploitation of one kind or another. This did not mean that money accumulation was limited to these august personages. The eighteenth century was a fine time for entrepreneurship in industry, in agriculture, in finance, in trade; and the opportunities opened up by Britain's expanding role in the world economy were not wasted.

As pointed out earlier, there were several routes to the accumulation of wealth. A man could inherit it, he could earn it in one way or another, or he could marry it.

Inheritance was the simplest, surest route to wealth. Most of the titled possessors of great wealth had begun with a healthy base of valuable property and assets left them by their families. Burlington, Chesterfield, Carlisle, and Leicester were only some of the more prominent of the nobles who were left well-succored by worldly goods. Inheritance was not limited to peers. Robert Child, for example, was left quite wealthy by his father, the famous banker, and William Baker founded his own spectacular commercial success on the comfortable estate bequeathed by his parents.

If one's father had not had the forethought to leave behind a substantial token of his affection, it was still possible to make money. As always, one of the more popular routes to wealth was through government office. Few were the men of wealth of this period who did not increase their net worth by holding office of one sort or another. Some of these officeholders, for example, Philip Dormer Stanhope, fourth Earl of Chesterfield, who held a variety of increasingly important offices from 1723 to 1748, earned their salaries and even steered clear of the temptation to line their pockets with bribes. The majority, however, must have more closely resembled the third Viscount Weymouth, later Marquess of Bath, who in 1765 was made Viceroy of Ireland and drew an annual salary of £16,000 plus an equipage allowance of £3,000 although he never went to Ireland and performed no duties.

If one's politics or lack of connections precluded a profitable public office, there was always industry as a source of wealth, a source plumbed by peer and commoner alike. Men of property could exploit mineral finds on their land holdings themselves or could—like the Duke of Norfolk, Lord Dudley, the Lawthers, the Lambtons, and the Delavals—lease the finds to industrialists for either rent or a cut of the gross production. An additional source of income came from their rental of right of way over their adjoining lands to the mine operators so that the minerals could be transported from the mines to a dock or depot.

One nobleman, the Duke of Bridgewater, recognized the need for improved transportation for minerals and other loads and employed James Brindley to construct a canal from Worsley to Manchester in 1759. The Bridgewater Canal proved a commercial success and a tribute to the business sagacity of its young initiator.

The eighteenth century was a good time to make money from industry—from mining, manufacturing, agriculture. The expanding English economy eagerly absorbed new products, whether they were good-quality porcelain or gaily patterned fabrics or any of the many other goods that were appearing in improved form. All the same, when we speak of an industrial revolution, we should keep in mind that the term may be misleading unless we realize that the phrase might be more accurately reworked to read a revolution in industry.

Industry itself was nothing particularly new. What was new in this century was, as C. Grant Robertson has noted, the "number and variety of inventions, the substitution of machinery for human power, the transition to organized production on a large scale." Particularly impressive was the number of inventions and discoveries.

In the textile field, the century saw the appearance of John Kay's flying shuttle, Paul and Wyatt's roller spinning, Hargreaves's spinning jenny, Arkwright's water frame, Cartwright's power loom, Murray's improved spinning frame and carding machine, and the wool-combing machines of Toplis, Hawksley, and Wright. This was also the era when John Lombe's successful purloining of the designs of the Italian silk-throwing machine in 1716 revolutionized the silk manufacturing industry.

In the iron and steel industry, Darby's and Cort's discoveries of processes allowing coal and coke to be substituted for charcoal in the refinement of pig iron opened almost limitless possibilities. Benjamin Huntsman, a Doncaster clockmaker, discovered a method in 1750 for making purer and harder steel, which made it possible for the Sheffield steelmakers to gain a manufacturing advantage that they would retain.

If a man were snobbish about staining his hands and mind with these pursuits, he could turn to agriculture, which was still the most-important industry in England. This was the century of the Enclosure Acts and the beginning of modern scientific farming. The Enclosure Acts, which increased steadily in numbers throughout the century, formed larger arable fields, creating opportunities for improved profits for great landowners while causing much hardship for tenant farmers and small freeholders.

Not content with the additional land made available for their use by the enclosures, wealthy landowners like Thomas Coke of Holkam were active in the reclamation of barren lands for farming. Over two-million new acres were created by reclamation during the century.

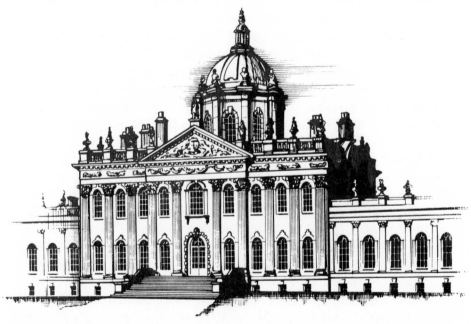

Castle Howard, Yorkshire: *The first major architectural effort by Sir John Vanbrugh, done 1700–1714 for his friend Lord Carlisle, Castle Howard is an effective representative of the English baroque school of Vanbrugh and Nicholas Hawksmoor, who also worked on the house.*

Agricultural innovations changed age-old techniques. There was an improved sowing system. "Turnip" Townshend fed turnips to live-stock during the winter, showing farmers that stock need not be slaughtered in the fall for lack of adequate winter food. Townshend also introduced the four-course rotation of wheat, barley, clover, and —of course—turnips. Several men explored the possibilities of the scientific breeding of cattle, most notably Thomas Bakewell.

The success of the agricultural innovations could be seen in the much-improved returns on the lands of the pioneers and in the fact that England not only fed itself, but also exported much of its wheat and dairy produce.

Trade was another source of revenue. Men of means invested heavily throughout the century in the great trading companies of the day: the South Sea Company, the East India Company, the Hudson's Bay Company. They also bought direct interests in one part or another of the growing empire. Investment in American lands was popular and often lucrative. British merchants who received government contracts for victualing and paying garrisons of British troops stationed throughout the empire found this international venture highly profitable, especially if they were not over-honest about giving value equivalent to the sums received under the contract.

The increasingly important financial institutions—the banks and the stock market—provided opportunities for men with wits and daring to wax fat off the misfortunes as well as the good fortune of the nation. Then, as now, manipulation was the name of the game, and the scandal concerning price manipulation of South Sea Company shares before the gigantic crash of 1720 led to a full-scale Parliamentary investigation and the rise to power of Robert Walpole.

Of all the ways to make money, possibly the most popular and certainly one of the most common was to marry it. It was no disgrace at all to repair or improve the family fortunes by seeking a great dowry. Young ladies of fortune, particularly those who were not themselves well born, doted on titles, leading characters like Vanbrugh's Sir Novelty to buy a better title to attract a richer bride. There were shadowy characters who made a business of acquainting the well-born and the well-dowered with their mutual attractions, or sometimes parents served in this role.

Young people could easily become the pawns of greedy and ambitious parents who would not hesitate to arrange a marriage totally unsuitable or even repugnant to the principals themselves to gratify their own desires. If not every such match endured the same painful history chronicled by Hogarth in *Marriage A La Mode*, these arrange-

ments must surely have encouraged the relatively casual marital relations of the time and led to much boredom if not actual suffering.

Young women were often powerless in these arrangements and
suffered the indignity of having their attractions gauged by their bank
accounts and their eligibility determined by their prospects. The best-
known plays of the time reflected the general callousness as far as
women and marriage were concerned. In George Farquhar's *The
Beaux Stratagem* (1706/7), Aimwell declares: "No woman can be a
beauty without a fortune." When Sir John Melvil changes his mind
about which sister he wishes to marry in the course of George Colman
and David Garrick's *The Clandestine Marriage* (1766), Sterling—
father of two girls—says understandingly that the change of heart does
not matter: "Since you only transfer from one girl to the other, it is
no more than transferring so much stock."

Marriage did not always, of course, involve a rich but ill-bred girl
and a great peer; sometimes the participants were social equals or
nearly so and the girl's dowry only a welcome bonus. Love was not
always missing from the nuptial vows, and romantic matches gleamed
all the more brightly for being so unusual among the rich and highly
born.

Often, marriages of convenience were between mature adults who
quite obviously knew what each would get from an alliance with the
other. After the marriage, the couple did not always go through even
the pretext of maintaining a joint establishment.

Inheriting, making, or marrying, there was a sizable body of men
who had one way or another got their hands on a great deal of money.
In keeping with the attitudes of the time about the fitness of a good
establishment, they did not shirk from spending their cash on the
creation of estates to be considered investments in political power
and social prestige as well as good financial risks.

There were, of course, men who allowed themselves to be unwisely
carried away by the mania for estate building. Even the wealthiest
of men sometimes overspent their current resources. Less well-to-do
imitators let their enthusiasm outstrip their purses, planning and
undertaking projects beyond their capacity. In his travels about England in the 1780s and 1790s, John Byng noted many country estates
in poor condition because their owners either could not or would
not devote adequate time and money to their maintenance or—in
some instances—completion.

The obsession with stability and posterity found lasting expression
in these great estates, many of which remain today in reasonably un-

altered form. The motives that directed men of means to build and furnish so sumptuously were not always of the highest, and the influences that operated on them were not always the most aesthetically desirable. And no serious student can accept some of the vague generalizations that one often encounters about the attractiveness of the leading lights of the period; many of the most-prominent estate builders were gross and unimaginative.

In spite of this, somehow it all works. Whatever the cause, the result was often magnificent, paying tribute even now to the general, perhaps unthinking acceptance of good design principles. If the average wealthy Georgian's success with architecture and decoration was merely an extension of his personal code of what was proper rather than evidence of an innate concern with art and the eternal verities, it is nonetheless apparent that his creation has in the eyes of the posterity with which he was so concerned far surpassed his intent.

The houses for which he bought the best works of some of the most-talented cabinetmakers of all time were a fitting framework for the pageant of eighteenth-century English civilization.

6

Habits, Hobbies, and the Changing Times

Lacquered or inlaid, carved or plain, Gothic or rococo, furniture must above all else be usable even if it is sometimes viewed as a work of art and only incidentally as a chair upon which we can sit or a table at which we can eat. As Goldsmith's imaginary Chinaman Lien Chi Altangi said: "Nothing is truly elegant but what unites use with beauty."

Practicality, that is, the demands of usage, may well be the single most-important influence on the furniture of any age. The activities and changing conditions of an era impose specific requirements on furniture. This was certainly true of eighteenth-century England. Such influences may be generally classed as those relating to (1) comfort and convenience and (2) pastimes.

For all its elegance and sense of proportion, the eighteenth century cannot have been very comfortable even for the wealthy. The imposing rooms that so delighted their aesthetic senses and buttressed their self-esteem must also have frozen their aristocratic toes. There was no central heating or use of stoves. Even blazing fires were inadequate in the large houses, a fact unpleasantly obvious to a Swedish visitor to London in February of 1748. The gentleman shiveringly noted that his wealthy host's drawing room was never warmer than 45 to 50 degrees.

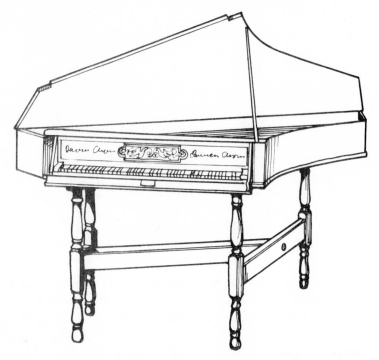

Queen Anne walnut spinet by Stephan Keene of London, ca. 1705.

Inadequate as fires may have been to heat whole rooms, they could loose unpleasantly hot blasts of air at anyone in their immediate vicinity. Protection from this possibility was afforded by fire screens meant to be placed before the hearth to shield anyone standing or sitting before the fire. Fire screens were small enough to be easily moved. The most popular fire screens, judging from the number that remain, were tripod poles supporting adjustable wood-framed embroidered panels. A more unusual and especially charming variety was the figural screen of the Queen Anne period. These figural screens were in the form of ladies in contemporary dress and were usually quite colorful. Cut of wood, sometimes oak, to match the full outline of a lady, the screen would then be painted with the proper details of face and dress. Ordinarily somewhat smaller than life size, the lady screens had backs grooved for attachment to a supporting stand.

Keeping the warmth of the fire contained was more of a problem than redirecting it. To this end, large folding screens remained popular. The best screens were very expensive, made of painted or incised Coromandel lacquer or of leather. Less-costly copies were sometimes decorated in the Chinese taste. Not easily moved because of their size and weight, these screens of six to twelve panels remained in the same general location to block the worst drafts and to keep the warmth of the fire from dissipating.

Drafts, cold, and damp were a special inconvenience in the bedroom. The gorgeous and voluminous bed hangings of the century could still serve quite effectively to creat an oasis of relative warmth about the bed. All the best pattern books of the time featured beds well endowed with canopy and draperies for this reason.

Not that it was always cold. Hot weather could also be a problem, and again the bedroom could be the room in which discomfort was most keenly felt. One attempt at solving this problem was made in Sheraton's design for an early version of twin beds. This very elegant bed had two compartments that shared the same four-poster frame, making it more comfortable for two people to share a bed in the hottest weather.

The concern for comfort extended to the contours of the human body. Gone for the most part were the hard, angular chairs and couches of earlier times. Chair backs acquired a faint but natural curve that supported the back without offense, and more-comfortable upholstery appeared on the seats and often the backs of both chairs and couches. These developments must have brought welcome relief to Georgian ladies imprisoned in their tightly laced bodices, yet determined to sit as gracefully as custom demanded.

A notable trend that intensified as the century progressed was the ever-increasing variety of furniture available. From the scanty furnishings of the Queen Anne house to the carefully coordinated interiors of Henry Holland, there had been a revolution in the kind and assortment of furniture deemed necessary for a well-furnished home. No longer could the fashionable householder get by with a few chairs, a settee, a few pictures, a looking glass, and a few shelves for the display of china in his drawing room. Inventive cabinetmakers were only too willing to abet this trend and to create a piece of furniture for every purpose.

The most-impressive proof of the variety of furniture available lay in what cabinetmakers advertised as their stock. There seemed no end to their virtuosity, as was seen in a representative listing of the 1730s, which included:

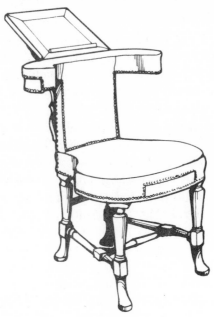

Queen Anne walnut reading chair with writing drawer and reading rest, ca. 1710.

Standing Beds and Bedding, large Glass Sconces in carv'd and gilt Frames, fine Wallnut-tree Desks and Book-Cases with Glass Doors, Wallnut-tree Double Chests of Drawers, Buroes, Buroe Tables, fine Wallnut-tree Quadrille Tables, Dressing Tables, several fine Mahogony Writing Tables on Casters, and new fashion'd Mahogony Tables which serve for five Uses, as Dining, Writing, Draughts, Backgammon, and Quadrille; Mahogony Tables and Breakfast Dining Tables, Night Tables, Box Tables, Corner Tables, and Dumb Waiters on casters, several fine Tables carv'd and gilt with Gold, several Dozens of the newest fashion'd Wallnut-tree Chairs, covered with Velvet, Damask, Black Spanish Leather, or uncover'd, fine Mahogony Chairs, Virginia Wallnut-tree Chairs with matted Bottoms, Beech Chairs of several sorts, fine Wallnut-tree Dressing Chairs, Close-Stool Chairs, Satees and Chair Beds, fine white Callicoe Quilts and Printed Quilts of all Sorts, fine new Whitney Blankets of all Sizes, Eight Day Clock Table Clocks, Carpets, Pictures, and China.

The emphasis of decoration shifted from the bedroom to the drawing room and other public reception rooms of the house. Better-designed, more-appealing chairs were produced in greater quantities to help fill this new need. Large display pieces were also introduced. The fashionable emphasis on reception rooms must have been responsible for the willingness of people of means to spend large sums of money on their decoration and furnishing, which in turn must have encouraged cabinetmakers to devise new designs for use in such rooms.

The dining room was the recipient of at least one completely new design, the sideboard. In the great houses, the dining room was usually some distance from the kitchen. This created obvious difficulties for both host and servants. To obviate these difficulties, Adam in the 1770s devised for Kenwood House a three-piece unit composed of a side table fitted between two pedestal cupboards topped with a metal-lined urn. One urn was for iced drinking water, the other for hot water to be used to wash up flat silver between courses. Sheraton later made this arrangement a one-piece unit. Another interesting article of dining-room furniture was the "set of tables," an extending dining table composed of several individual tables which fitted together to form a whole. The set of tables did away with the need for ponderously large dining tables and allowed for more freedom of placement when the whole table was not in use.

Other articles of furniture found in the well-furnished dining room might include dumbwaiters, wine coolers, cellarets, and side tables. After 1770, storage pieces began to appear. The dumbwaiter, whose construction was made possible by the introduction of mahogany, was a three-tiered tray that stood at the side of the diner's chair so that he could help himself from its revolving trays. Used either for lack of servants or the wish for privacy impossible when the help was present, dumbwaiters were not usually found in the best dining rooms. The large numbers of wine coolers and cellarettes that were made attested to the popularity of wine drinking, and these items were very useful for serving and storing wine in the dining room itself. As in earlier times, side tables continued much in evidence.

George II walnut stool, on cabriole legs with carved shell design on the knees and with pad feet, the upholstery in embroidery, ca. 1730–1750.

Palladian architecture had a decided effect on furniture usage. Windows, for example, tended to be few and narrow in relation to wall expanse. To fill in the plain, narrow wall space between these tall sash windows, furniture designers suggested side tables or console tables with large looking glasses hanging above. These pier tables and glasses were often made in pairs because many eighteenth-century rooms were planned with three windows on a wall, necessitating two tables and glasses for the piers between the windows.

One of the most-obvious changes in interior decoration was the increased importance of mirrors. The vistas so integral to the concept of Palladianism were much enhanced by proper placement of looking glasses. It would be difficult to overestimate the striking effects created by the lavish use of the elegantly framed mirrors. Many eighteenth-century rooms without them would have seemed like a beautiful face without eyebrows—devoid of expression.

Another influence exerted by architecture operated on bed designs. As rooms got larger and taller, beds got taller and received more decorative attention.

The new emphasis on liveliness in all parts of room decoration altered the complexion of an old trade. The leather gilders found themselves becoming paperhangers who usually functioned also as decorators. Firms like Thomas Bromwich's and Crompton & Spinnage transformed drawing rooms, bedrooms, any rooms into the desired mood—be it Chinese, Gothic, or simply sumptuous—with fantastic wallpapers and made-to-order rugs.

With the waning of Palladianism and the rise of neoclassicism, the affinity between furniture and architecture became even more pronounced. Between 1760 and 1800 architect and cabinetmaker worked more closely together than ever before. The most-extreme example of this collaboration was Henry Holland's designing of certain articles of furniture to be built into the rooms of his houses.

At times, of course, the occupants of the well-decorated houses journeyed outside their own walls, outside even the country, and this well-bred traveling had its own influence on furniture design. Fastidious men and women of means liked comfort and did not like bedbugs, sentiments that prompted them to carry portable chair-beds with them when they traveled. Soldiers, those enforced travelers, had to carry their own equipment with them at this time. On receiving his commission early in the century, one young officer wrote that before leaving for the Continent he must procure: "a tent, a bed, a baggage

George II mahogany kneehole writing table on six cabriole legs, ca. 1745.

horse and a gold sash." The gold sash was vanity, but the bed was a necessity unless the soldier intended sleeping on the ground.

Ships became much more numerous during this century, and there was a brisk trade in furnishing them attractively and well without sacrificing practicality. Ship furniture, usually made of mahogany, was designed for hard wear and was often very handsome, though lacking the elegant touches found in the best landbound work.

People of means who were emigrating or at least planning a lengthy visit to some distant part of the empire could buy a variety of furniture to make their jaunt more homelike. There were firms like Morgan and Sanders who specialized in compact, portable furniture—dining tables that would seat over twenty people then fold to a very small size; portable chairs so compact that a dozen would pack in the same space as two ordinary chairs; sofa beds that could be transformed into complete four-poster beds; chair beds that looked like easy chairs and could be made up into a tent bed; and portable beds that were easily assembled and disassembled without tools.

Transporting furniture, compact or otherwise, to distant lands was usually accomplished by renting only space on a ship, that is, renting an unfurnished cabin, using one's own furniture to furnish the cabin, then removing it at the end of the voyage.

Most people stayed at home, save for occasional jaunts to Europe, and the large number of practicing cabinetmakers were not slow to grasp the fact that their clients would pay very nice prices for furniture that fulfilled their exact needs and desires. Style and appearance were important, but so was purpose.

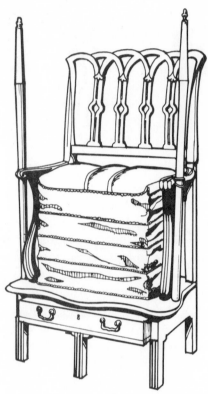

George III mahogany chamber-horse, with detachable chair back and exercise grips, ca. 1760.

The dressing table, for example, developed out of the passion that both men and women of the time had for primping. Most people of fashion were quite vain and prized personal appearance as much as any other form of beauty. Both sexes used dressing tables although those for men tended to be more severe and less ornate than those for women. In "Gratitude" (1786) poet William Cowper describes the luxurious accoutrements of his life as providing an excellent setting for indulging his "poetical moods," Paying particular attention to:

This table and mirror within,
Secure from collision and dust,
At which I oft shave cheek and chin,
And periwig nicely adjust.

The concern with physical appearance extended to the question of weight. In a time when even the most-abstemious nobleman could scarcely avoid what we would consider an inordinate amount of rich eating and drinking, being overweight was a fairly widespread problem. Overfed squires were the norm not the exception, and an unusual piece of furniture was developed for people with weight problems. The "chamber–horse" was a mechanical aid used by the overweight wanting to lose some of their excess pounds.

Although first recorded by Thomas Sheraton in the third revised edition of *The Cabinet-maker and Upholsterer's Drawing Book* (1802), the chairs—also known as dandy horses and riding chairs, presumably because they simulated the movement of horseback riding—had been made since mid-century, having probably been invented by Henry March of Clement's Inn Passage, Clare-Market. Some of the

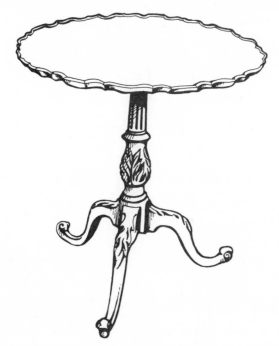

George III mahogany tripod table, often used for tea, with scroll feet and a pie crust top, ca. 1760.

chairs were in the form of exercise stools; others had chair backs. The seat was made up of several layers of heavy coils encased in leather. The would-be exerciser sat on the seat and bounced his avoirdupois up and down to force the coils to contract, rather like an early form of isometrics.

Not all articles of furniture specially ordered by the wealthy for personal use were rooted in vanity. In 1751 the proud Burlington must have found it very galling to order a special "machine chair" from William Hallett when he could no longer get around easily.

When they were not bouncing about on their chamber–horses, Englishmen and women had many other pastimes to occupy their time and purses. The range of popular pastimes was large, encompassing such diverse activities as gaming and needlework, and each activity encouraged the development of new furniture forms.

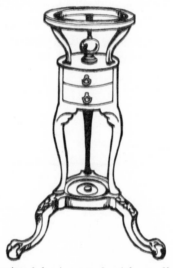

George III mahogany tripod basin stand with scroll supports and two small drawers and boasting ball-and-claw feet, ca. 1770.

Perhaps the most widely spread hobby of the day was gambling, if we can call so ubiquitous a mania a mere hobby. The upper classes were crazy about gambling throughout the century, a fondness they shared with several of their monarchs, especially the thoroughly respectable Queen Anne. In 1700 Lady Mary Coke wrote to her husband from the then Princess Anne's court:

> Her Highness . . . was extremely civil, and offered me a stool to sit down and play at basset; but I refused and told her I durst not venture for fear of loving it too well.

Lady Mary was wise, for many did love basset too well, along with ombre, picquet, whisk, brag, and lanterloo. Bankruptcy was the reward of several nobles and their ladies who were too fond of gambling. In 1725 Lady Mary Wortley Montagu wrote to her sister that:

> The discreet and sober Lady Lechmere has lost such Furious summs at the Bath that 'tis question'd whether all the sweetness that the Waters can put into my Lord's blood can make him endure it, particularly 700 pounds at one sitting.

The unfortunate Lady L. subsequently piled up gambling debts of between five- to ten-thousand pounds. When her husband balked at paying, she attempted suicide, but failed, having no better luck than she had enjoyed at the gaming tables.

A lady could lose more than pounds while gambling, for it was during a tea break from a game of ombre that Pope's fair Belinda lost the ill-fated, favorite lock of hair to "the conqu'ring force of unresisted steel." Pope based "The Rape of the Lock" on an actual incident involving some of his well-born friends.

George III four-poster bed with inlaid satinwood columns, the cornice being pierced, carved and decorated, with ample bed hangings, in the manner of Adam, ca. 1770.

Women were not the only victims of the gaming tables. White's, a fashionable gambling club on St. James's in London, was a favorite haunt of most of the wealthiest noblemen and commoners (as well as a few tolerably bred card sharks) of the day. Once ensconced within the walls of this inner sanctum of chance, members would bet on anything: cards, love, motherhood, war, even the weather. Their daring did not come cheap. Lord Carlisle lost £10,000 in one night. The worldly Earl of Chesterfield, so wise in all ways save this one, depleted his personal fortune in play.

The all-engrossing gaming led to the perfection and numerous manufacture of various styles of game tables, many of which could be folded and placed against the wall for the sake of convenience. Most of the earlier gaming tables had counter wells to hold chips and money at each corner or—if the table were round—spaced for four players, but later tables dispensed with this feature.

Not all nobles and men of wealth spent all their time at the tables. Many of them read a good deal, and there was an impressive number of private libraries in England. Almost all of the so-called "building Earls" had fine libraries and included plans for sumptuous fittings to house them when constructing their homes. Chesterfield considered his library to be the greatest in England and the star of his exquisite

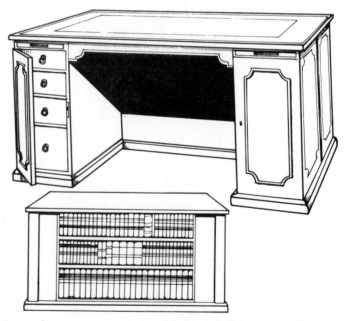

George III mahogany center desk with bookshelves, ca. 1780.

Chesterfield House. Thomas Coke, later first Earl of Leicester, was an ardent bibliophile all his life, much of which he spent accumulating his collection of architectural books and drawings. Edward Harley, second Earl of Oxford, son of the great politician Robert Harley, shared his father's love of books and assembled one of the most-inclusive libraries of the century, part of which was purchased in the 1750s by the government for the newly established British Museum.

All these books suggest a passion for reading, and this led to the design of at least one new piece of furniture: the straddling chair. This chair was meant to be straddled while one rested one's arms on the rounded, padded top of its relatively low back. In the center of the back was a book rest and at each side a sconce for a candle. Some examples had a swingout box in each arm rest for pens and ink. Not all reading chairs were meant to be straddled, and another object of Cowper's "Gratitude" was:

> This wheel-footed studying chair,
> Contrived both for toil and repose,
> Wide-elbow'd, and wadded with hair
> In which I both scribble and doze,
> Bright-studded to dazzle the eyes,
> And rival in lustre of that
> In which, or astronomy lies,
> Fair Cassiopeia sat.

Book collecting required large storage pieces. The damp could harm precious volumes, so it was preferable that these pieces have doors of glass or wood. Bookcases and breakfronts became larger and more elaborate towards the middle of the century, and often replaced old-fashioned fitted shelves in libraries, a fact possibly responsible for their retention of an architectural treatment in construction and ornamentation. The weight of these pieces led to the widespread use of casters or "swivells."

Scribbling was another popular hobby of the time. While not always concerned with indulging "poetical fancies" on paper, upper-class Englishmen and women of this century were rabid letter writers, as the many collections of letters still extant prove. The variety of desks to be had was impressive. Large or small, ornate or plain, the desk could be a simple, one-purpose article of furniture or one part of another piece, such as a secrétaire or a bureau. There were few rooms that did not contain some sort of desk. John Cobb invented a new kind of desk meant for the convenience of draftsmen or others who needed or who wished to stand while they worked.

Women apparently read little, and most who did probably confined themselves to light, sentimental novels; but almost all leisured women did needlework. Queen Mary had encouraged the popularity of needlework in the 1690s by using it copiously for decorative purposes after the prevailing style in France. Gentlewomen took up embroidery with a passion. It was a socially acceptable, as well as a useful hobby and gave one a chance to exhibit skill.

George III satinwood Beau Brummel, serpentine front crossbanded with rosewood; the top drawer fitted with adjustable mirror and boxes, ca. 1785.

One noblewoman wrote in 1725 of a typical day: "I work like an angel, I receive visits upon Idle days, and shade my Life as I do my Tent stitch." Debating whether or not to leave London for her country place, she later sighed: "Tis all one to me whether I see Beasts cover'd with their natural Hides, or Embroidierys."

She would have seen "Beasts" on stools or pole fire screens or covering the tops of small card tables, all favored pieces to display needlework.

Music had its wealthy admirers. Some played themselves, and others patronized deserving musicians and musical endeavors. The Earl of Burlington actually played the harpsichord and rented one to accompany him on part of his Grand Tour through Italy. It was a hobby that he kept throughout his life. While not many noblemen played, the harpsichord was not an uncommon item of furnishing in their houses.

Cabinetmakers furnished very elegant cases for harpsichords so that they could sit comfortably in the grand houses for which many of

George III mahogany triple top games table in the manner of the 1740s, ca. 1780–1790.

them were made. Mechanical organs also enjoyed a vogue. In 1735 Benjamin Goodison made a case for a mechanical organ and harpsichord for Kensington Palace, along with a set of nine dwarf cabinets to hold the organ rolls. Unfortunately, this case was later altered by William Vile to make an ordinary cabinet.

One of the outstanding characteristics of wealthy Georgians was their interest in collecting. Since the late seventeenth century, the upper classes had collected curios—jewels, coins, medals. In the eighteenth century, collecting was extended to include other objects, especially import china. Again, Queen Mary had led the way with her impressive collection of oriental porcelain and Delft ware which she displayed on side tables and open shelves. This method of display had obvious flaws, and it was not long before cabinetmakers were creating various sorts of cabinets and cases—usually open shelved or glass-fronted—to hold collections. The importance of display pieces increased with the growing popularity of the tea ritual, which called for a wide variety of porcelain that needed to be stored and displayed when not in actual use. The small china cabinet was one of the most-appealing results of this desire for usable storage pieces that would look well in reception rooms.

The avid collecting of pictures that was such a prominent feature

George III mahogany sideboard, with brass rails, in the manner of Sheraton, ca. 1785–1795.

of the entire period necessitated a lively trade in frames, usually heavily carved and gilded, that made a brilliant addition to the already colorful rooms in which they were hung.

Not all collections were inanimate. Queen Charlotte liked fish, and in 1762 William Vile made for the monarch a goldfish bowl stand, complete with "a neat mahogany handle to a Fish net."

The ritual of tea was possibly the single most-potent influence on decoration. Beyond the large amounts of porcelain and other accessories required for the well–bred consumption of the exotic, expensive beverage, there was suddenly a need for a steady table of the right size to hold all this paraphernalia. Some houses gave each tea drinker his own individual table. Unsteadiness was a particular problem on the uneven floors of most houses, thus tripod bases were good for tea tables. Elegance was another desirable quality. This ritual required more than mere utilitarianism. The ritualistic feel of tea drinking was captured by Pope in "The Rape of the Lock" when Belinda and her crafty suitor interrupt their card play to partake of tea:

> For lo! the board with cups and spoons is crown'd,
> The Berries crackle, and the mill turns round;
> On shining altars of Japan they raise,
> The sliver lamp; the fiery spirits blaze:
> From silver spouts the grateful liquors glide,

While China's earth receives the smoking tide,
At once they gratify their scent and taste,
And frequent cups prolong the rich repast.

As this brief survey indicates, a striking feature of the eighteenth century was the proliferation of the sorts of furniture deemed essential to the furnishing of a fashionable house. Since London townhouses rarely had the ampleness of space found in great country places, there was a demand for furniture which would attractively serve a dual purpose. A secrétaire might double as a dressing table, and practically every standing cabinet piece doubled as a desk. One interesting combination article perfected at this time was the press bedstead, an ingenious wardrobe that contained a bed. Its purpose was to save space and to provide extra sleeping accomodation. Inns often had such pieces, and so did the Duke of Newcastle. Newcastle, reputedly afraid of the dark, had one in his bedroom for his footman.

George III work box on stand, made of satinwood inlaid with swags of hare-wood and boxwood, ca. 1790.

As life became more complicated and ordinary men and women of wealth developed broader interests, furniture had to develop new forms. Cabinetmakers met this requirement in many styles without falling into the trap of novelty for its own sake.

One of the most-piquant aspects of eighteenth-century English furniture was the care lavished on even the most-insignificant dumbwaiter and the restraint usually evident in even the most intricate of dressing tables. Cabinetmakers responded well to the dictates of habits, hobbies, and the changing times, retaining their highly developed sense of proportion and producing articles of furniture possessing a certain integrity however narrow or frivolous their intended use.

7

The Exotic and the Distant

I*t* is misleading to speak of foreign or historical influences as if they
were exceptional, if by so doing we imply that design is ever entirely
free from these influences. It is far more accurate simply to assess
which particular influence is predominant at a given time and in what
way it affects domestic design. This was especially so of eighteenth-
century English furniture. There were very few articles of fine furniture produced in England during the century that owed no debt
to one or more of these influences. By their shape, their carving, their
ornamentation, or the treatment of their materials, most articles of
furniture betrayed a touch not purely of contemporary English origin.

If this had not been so, it would have been surprising; for even in
the days before modern communication the educated world shared
certain aspects of culture. Decoration, that plaything of fashion, was
especially susceptible to new influences whatever their source, and fads
in decoration exerted an all-important influence on furniture design.

In some ways English furniture design of this century owed a direct
debt to foreign influences. The cabriole leg, probably derived from the
goat's leg, came from China and Egypt by way of Italy, Holland, and
France. Also in China originated the ball-and-claw foot in the form of
a three-clawed dragon holding the sacred pearl, symbolizing the protection of purity and integrity from evil demons. The practice of

making chair backs more comfortable by bending them slightly came from China. From France came several articles of furniture to be added to the English cabinetmakers' repertoire: the console table, the commode, the chest of drawers, the corner cupboard, and the chiffonier. It was the work of French makers that popularized the use of upholstery on the backs, as well as the seats of chairs and couches. Marquetry, inlay, and the fashion for lacquered decoration were Dutch contributions, as was the burgomaster chair, direct ancestor of the English writing chair with its solid wood back, large comfortable seat, and wide arm rests. In fact, the Dutch craftsmen who came to England after the accession of William and Mary were the single-greatest influence on English furniture design in the late Stuart period.

For the most part, foreign and historical influences on English furniture were more subtle and, perhaps for that reason, more pervasive. The major design influences of the eighteenth century in England were the Chinese, the Palladian, the Gothic, the rococo, and the neoclassical revival. To give exact dates to any of these styles is arbitrary, for there was much overlapping and even intermingling of designs. Generally speaking, however, Chinese influences were important from the beginning of the century to 1730 and from 1745 to 1765; Palladian from 1720 to 1750; Gothic from 1740 to 1770; rococo from 1745 to 1765; and the neoclassical revival from 1760 to the end of the century.

The Chinese was the most exotic of the important foreign influences. By Chinese I do not mean so much the direct influence of contact with a wide variety of Chinese customs and products, but rather the *idea* that most eighteenth-century Englishmen had of China.

China was not, even to the man of average education and travel experience, a geographic entity lying within a certain longitude and latitude; it was Cathay, a fabled land so strange and different as to boggle the Western mind. That their map of Cathay had been platted by imaginative voyagers, both actual and chair bound, rather than by topographers did not deter Englishmen and other Westerners from believing that they knew all about this distant earthly paradise.

The whimsical landscape of Cathay was as well known to them as was their own street, and the quaint figures populating the landscape as familiar as the people of the next town. Eighteenth-century Englishmen knew that Cathay was a magnificent place where endless wealth was spent to create a setting of barbaric splendor. In this opulent, yet somehow fiitting and therefore tasteful environment throve a way of life that seemed superior in many ways to that of eighteenth-century

Europe. A just and humane administration enveloped its grateful subjects with benevolence, and allowed them leisure to contemplate the
beautiful. The only flaw in this wondrous place was the occasional
fire-breathing dragon that was almost as quaint as the peasant that it
threatened.

Queen Anne red lacquer bureau cabinet, decorated in gold and black chinoiserie, ca. 1700–1705.

It is an interesting facet of human nature that most people want a
never-never land in which to believe, a place far beyond the boundaries
of their experience and far above the mundane trivia with which their

own lives seem surfeited. Cathay was tailor-made for this purpose. The few genuine travelers' accounts of it—Marco Polo's in the fourteenth century was the first published—emphasized the fantastic and the unexpected. So basic and so massive were Western misconceptions about the East that it was five hundred years before the breathless, monster-ridden *The Travels of Sir John Mandeville* was revealed as a total fraud, the wholesale invention of a man who had never traveled beyond the Mediterranean. The most successful nonreligious book of the medieval era, *Sir John Mandeville* was translated into ten languages during the centuries before its true origin was revealed.

The free communication that would have laid the myths to rest was impossible because the Chinese government stringently controlled all intercourse between China and the outside world. The occasional trade, diplomatic, and religious contacts sanctioned by the government were so limited that they allowed only a tantalizing glimpse of Chinese life and thus kept alive Western interest in China without subjecting it to the test of reality.

Since there was very little factual information to contradict it, the image of China as Cathay lingered relatively undisturbed. For centuries, China sporadically intrigued educated Westerners, and its culture seemed quite worthy of imitation. The easiest form of imitation was to adopt some of the trappings of Chinese decoration. Since few Englishmen could go to China, their idea of Chinese decoration was hazy at best; but this did not keep them from wanting and buying goods in the Chinese taste, including furniture.

As early as the late sixteenth century some Englishmen of wealth had accumulated small collections of genuine Chinese porcelain, but the first real craze for the Chinese style in England came during the Restoration period and was heavily influenced by the style's popularity at the court of Louis XIV. From 1700 to the 1730s there remained fashionable a definite Chinese style that had been transmitted to England by Dutch craftsmen in the late seventeenth century. This style did not affect the form of furniture, only its finish. If a client wanted something Chinese, his cabinetmaker merely lacquered the selected item and decorated it with chinoiserie. Chinoiserie, the European interpretation of oriental motifs seen on real Chinese imports of porcelain, fabrics and furniture, featured oddly proportioned figures against a fanciful background inhabited by miraculous beasts and marvelous plant life. This lacquered finish, known as *japan,* was applied to all sorts of furniture from minute card tables to large secrétaires.

Japanned furniture had tumbled from the height of fashion by the 1720s and by the 1730s was no longer considered stylish except as a craft hobby indulged in by ladies of quality, but the taste for chinoiserie was never entirely sated. When the graceful bombé of Louis XV furniture began infiltrating England in the 1740s, its lines seemed to call for the added touch of chinoiserie decoration. Soon, this was not enough for devotees of the Chinese cult, and for the first time chinoiserie went beyond surface decoration to affect carving and shape. Sharp angularity and pierced backs reminiscent of the framing of chinoiserie bridges began to characterize chairs and settees in the Chinese style. Wood carved to simulate bamboo made legs for all sorts of furniture. Pediments of cabinets and secrétaires sometimes sported pierced carving.

In the mid-1750s French rococo softened this angularity and added its curves and fancies to the English Chinese style. Even Gothic motifs, especially the pointed arch, had an effect on the style.

The resulting eclecticism was sometimes bizarre, usually picturesque, often beautiful, and always interesting. Considering the attractiveness of chinoiserie furniture and decoration and the fashionableness of the

George II carved and gilded term torchère, probably designed by William Kent and made by Benjamin Goodison, showing baroque feel of much Palladian furniture, ca. 1730.

Chinese style, it was not surprising that some Englishmen went overboard for Chinese. They decorated their walls with chinoiserie stucco work or hung them with chinoiserie-printed wallpaper. They filled their rooms with a symphony of angular or curved, lacquered or pierced chinoiserie furniture. They ate and drank from chinoiserie-decorated porcelain. They collected japanned boxes. They went to costume balls in mandarin dress, and their demand for chinoiserie went beyond the adornment of their persons and the interiors of their houses. Their gardens spouted Chinese outbuildings; Chinese fretwork bridges spanned their streams. Duke William Augustus of Cumberland, the second son of George II, built a yacht decorated in the Chinese manner.

The vogue for Chinese went to such lengths that satirists were quick to seize the opportunity to score. In 1755 there appeared John Shebbeare's *Letters on the English Nation: By Battista Angeloni, a Jesuit, Who resided many years in London,* in which it was found that:

> The simple and sublime have lost all influence almost everywhere, all is Chinese or Gothic; every chair in an apartment, the frames of glasses and tables, must be Chinese; the walls covered with Chinese paper filled with figures which resemble nothing of God's creation, and which a prudent nation would prohibit for the sake of pregnant women.

> In one chamber, all the pagods and distorted animals of the east are piled up, and called the beautiful decorations of a chimneypiece; on the sides of the room, lions made of porcelain, grinning and misshapen, are placed on brackets of the Chinese taste, in arbors of flowers made in the same ware, and leaves of grass painted green lying like lovers in the shades of old Arcadia.

> Nay, so excessive is the love of Chinese architecture become, that at present the fox hunters would be sorry to break a leg in pursuing their sport in leaping any gate that was not made in the eastern taste of little bits of wood standing in all directions; the connoisseurs of the table delicacies can distinguish between the taste of an ox which eats his hay from a Chinese crib, a hog that is inclosed in a stye of that kind, or a fowl fattened in a coop the fabric of which is in that design, and find great difference in the flavor.

In 1756 James Cawthorn's "Of Taste" poked fun at the fad in verse:

> Of late, 'tis true, quick sick of Rome and Greece
> We fetch our models from the wise Chinese:
> European artists are too cool and chaste,
> For Mand'rin is the only man of taste . . .
> On ev'ry shelf a Joss divinely stares,
> Nymphs laid on chintzes sprawl upon our chairs,

While o'er our cabinets Confucius nods,
Midst porcelain elephants and China gods.

The most successful of the satires was the series of 119 "Chinese Letters" published in John Newbury's *Public Ledger* in 1760–1761. Purporting to be the observations of a Chinese visitor in London, the letters were in reality the work of Oliver Goldsmith, who was paid £100 per year for his comic efforts.

Not content with Chinese decoration alone, patrons read chinoiserie literature like the frequently reprinted *OEconomy of Human Life,* a 1750 book posing as a Tibetan guide to duty which transferred the aspect of Anglican deism to the Chinese, and Thomas Percy's translation from the French of *Hau Kiou Choaan,* a Chinese novel. Garrick's production of Noverre's ballet *The Chinese Festival* (1755) did not fare as well. In spite of sumptuously chinoiserie sets, its French dancers were forced from the stage by antigallicans pelting them with rotten apples. Arthur Murphy's *The Orphan of China* (1759), also produced by Garrick, probably utilizing the sets of *The Chinese Festival,* was quite successful.

The Chinese custom that was to have the most lasting effect on English life was the drinking of tea, which introduced many specialized articles and pieces of furniture and influenced the decoration of drawing rooms. Tea drinking, hitherto endured for medicinal purposes, had become fashionable following Catherine of Braganza's marriage to Charles II in 1662. The Portugese Infanta who had become Queen of England convinced the court of the more-pleasurable aspects of tea, and began a practice which required its own paraphernalia and about which developed a distinct social ritual. Although expensive, the habit of tea became a required part of civilized life in eighteenth-century England and undoubtedly caused many returns to the Chinese taste because it was a constant and pleasant reminder of the Chinese civilization.

Reflections of the widespread interest in the Chinese were to be found in some tradesmen's cards featuring drawings of elegant chairs in the Chinese Chippendale manner and fretwork-decorated tea tables and advertising "the greatest Variety of nice Tea-Tables, Trays and Chests." The best cabinetmakers were naturally affected by the Chinese style since their fashion-conscious clients demanded that their furniture reflect the latest trends. Because of *The Director's* successful chinoiserie designs, the name of Thomas Chippendale has been assigned to most furniture in this style, but there were other cabinetmakers and carvers who were well known for Chinese productions.

George II carved and gilded console in the English rococo style, with a white-veined orange marble top; the Chinese figures sculpted in full relief and sitting in a bower composed of natural and abstract motifs, ca. 1755–1760.

William Hallett, one of the most important adherents to the style at mid-century, had the distinction of having no less fastidious a critic than Horace Walpole dismiss his creations as "mongrel Chinese." The great neoclassicist Robert Adam executed oriental designs when ordered by Sarah Jodrell Child, the wife of wealthy banker Robert Child. Sarah, who was quite fond of the oriental taste, had commissioned Adam to redesign the dressing room, drawing room, the china and japan after chambers, possibly the Long Gallery, and probably the Tapestry Room at Osterley in the 1770s; and their faint oriental flavor proved how effectively Cathay's influence lingered. The severe Sheraton was not immune. As late as 1795, he designed a chair to be turned in wood to simulate bamboo and to be lacquered in brown, then decorated in gold chinoiserie.

Both architectural and furniture pattern books capitalized on the interest in Chinese designs. The first pattern book to show Chinese influence was William Halfpenny's *New Designs for Chinese Temples*

(1750). It was rapidly followed by Darly's *A New Book of Chinese, Gothic & Modern Chairs,* Darly and Edwards's *A New Book of Chinese Designs Calculated to Improve the Present Taste,* Chippendale's *The Director,* Chambers's *Designs of Chinese Buildings, Furniture, Dresses, Machines and Utensils,* Johnson's *Collection of Designs,* Halfpenny's *Chinese & Gothic Architecture properly ornamented,* Over's *Architecture in the Gothic, Chinese and Modern Taste,* and Decker's *Chinese Architecture, Civil and Ornamental.* In few of these many designs was there any attempt to go beyond chinoiserie to an indication of genuinely Chinese elements of design.

It is in the pages of these pattern books that we can see most clearly the English tendency to amalgamate chinoiserie with Gothic and rococo elements, and the degree of success attending these amalgamations indicates the basically fantastic quality of these influences.

And what was the attitude of the Chinese themselves towards the Englishmen and other Europeans whose "Chinese" furniture designs so little resembled the much-simpler Chinese furniture? According to Richard Walter's published account (1748) of Lord Anson's voyage around the world, the Chinese considered Westerners barbarians. Although the book had reached its fifteenth edition by 1780, having presumably been read by a relatively large audience, most Westerners did not seem perturbed by the judgment, clinging tenaciously to at least one manifestation of the Chinese style until the end of the century. "Chinese" furniture might begin to pall, but Englishmen seemingly never tired of their Anglo-Chinese gardens.

The key characteristic of these gardens, their planned informality, did not originate in China, but the gardens used certain Chinese elements—fretwork bridges and pagodas and, in one instance, a Chinese dairy (built in 1787 by Henry Holland at Woburn). Humphrey Repton, the prominent landscape architect, was particularly fond of the pleasing aspect of Chinese buildings nestling in the midst of English parks.

France was the most-influential country in the artistic world of the eighteenth century, setting the example for most of fashionable Europe. Of all European countries, England was least affected by the craze for French styles; even so, French influences had been felt in England long before rococo crossed the Channel in the 1740s.

French policy towards Huguenots had forced most of those who could to leave France during the seventeenth century, and many of the émigrés went to England, taking their often valuable skills with them. The Huguenot craftsmen offered a welcome injection of liveliness to English arts, which were not slow to respond. Huguenot weavers, for example, helped to consolidate the position of the Spital-fields textile industry, which enjoyed its greatest success in the early Georgian era.

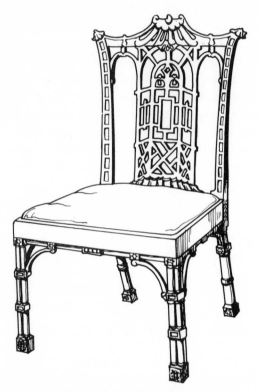

George III mahogany side chair in the Chinese taste, ca. 1760.

The turn of the eighteenth century saw at least two prominent French craftsmen influencing English design: Jean Tijou and Daniel Marot. Tijou, a designer of ironwork, worked with English architect William Talman on such showplaces as Hampton Court, Chatsworth, Burghley, and Drayton. In 1693 he had published *A new Booke of Drawings,* the earliest English ironwork book, and his very lush style, notable for its lavish use of acanthus scrolls, had an indirect effect on later English design.

A more-direct influence was exerted by Marot, a French architect who had fled the Terror to Holland, where he agreed to work for William III in England. The work of Marot, who designed both houses and suites of furniture, incorporated both the French and Dutch styles later popularized by his design book that was published in Amsterdam in 1712. Perhaps Marot's most lasting contribution to English design was the influence that his work exerted on arch-Palladian William Kent.

Early French influence was not confined to designers. Gerrit Jensen, cabinetmaker to three English monarchs beginning in 1689, was known to have direct contacts with Paris and utilized French techniques in making his unusual metal marquetry furniture. French born John Pelletier worked as a cabinetmaker in England during the first decade of the century.

Gesso, the gayest early eighteenth–century English furniture, owed both its surface and ornamentation to French inspiration. The technique itself was Continental, and the shell and pendant husk so popular for gesso ornament were imports from France. French influence was indeed apparent in almost all designs for gesso ornament, and the best English craftsmen specializing in gesso—James Moore, for example—revealed an obvious dependence on the French designers whose engraved works were issued in England between 1700 and 1720.

One reason for the eighteenth-century French ascendancy in the decorative arts was the French appetite for the novel; but there was one style that seemed to capture most perfectly the aristocratic and pleasure-seeking atmosphere of the times—the rococo. The natural reaction of the court of Louis XV against the pompousness of the last years of the Sun King led to the acceptance of this less-serious, more-delicate, and more-voluptuous style of decoration, of which chinoiserie was one manifestation.

Juste Aurèle Meissonier, appointed designer to Louis XV in 1724, might be called the catalytic agent for rococo, as his widely circulated engravings disseminated the new style throughout Europe. Meissonier's extravagant rococo made liberal use of the shell motif later adopted so successfully by English carvers. The graceful scroll foot was another of his favorite devices for furniture. His designs for tapestries provided one of the most-charming expressions of the rococo.

It was in silver that the rococo found its first and possibly its happiest English home. Silversmiths, such as the Huguenot Paul de Lamerie, spearheaded the French rococo attack on the decorative arts of England. It was not long before English furniture designers began to take note.

With the advent of mahogany, the English attraction to the less-flamboyant elements of French design could be realized in wood carving and in the shape of furniture. The serpentine and the bow began to appear occasionally in English work, as did the alluring curves of the continental designs. By 1738 the English taste for French styles had become prevalent enough to warrant *The London Magazine's* complaining of the "Extravagancy of *following* the French *Fashions* . . . I mean the ridiculous Imitation of the *French,* which is now become the epidemical Distemper of this Kingdom."

English interest in the naturalistic ornament of French rococo soon revealed itself in furniture pattern books. In 1740 Batty and Thomas Langley included in *The City and Country Builder's and Workman's Treasury of Designs* drawings for six rococo console tables. Although these designs were plagiarized from decorative designs of Nicholas Pineau, the French wood carver who had worked for Peter the Great early in the eighteenth century, the Langleys failed to acknowledge any indebtedness to the French craftsman.

It was also in 1740 that Matthias Lock produced *A New Drawing Book of Ornaments, Shields, Compartments, Masks, etc.* Lock, a well-established carver, had no need to copy French models, using them instead as a basis for his own interpretation of the rococo. Lock's approach to rococo was more successful than that of French artist De La Cour, then at work in England, who published his own rather-awkward rococo designs during this decade. Lock's *Six Sconces* (1744) and *Six Tables* (1746) marked a turning point in English rococo, for Lock adapted the style for actual articles of furniture to be carved. H. Copland's *A New Book of Ornaments* (1746) showed his artistic skill, and in 1752 Lock and Copland collaborated on *A New Book of Ornaments with twelve leaves,* a revolutionary work which incorporated designs for a wide range of furniture to be carved. In this book Lock and Copland demonstrated the anglicization of French rococo and, incidentally, introduced the element of chinoiserie into carving, the first published design to do so.

At mid-century the French influence remained the most potent in Europe and was so strong in Italy that gentleman-student Robert Adam, happily engaged in contemplating classical ruins and buying old prints, remarked: "The Italians have at present no manner of taste, all they do being more French than anything else." In England, under the patronage of the Duke of Cumberland, a shortlived Westminster workshop was set up in 1750 by two French weavers formerly of Savonnerie to produce tapestry in the French style.

In English furniture, the French rococo was to see the height of its popularity in the 1750s. Designs in Chippendale's *The Director* in the rococo manner featured scroll feet terminating elegant cabriole legs and ribbon-interlaced chair backs. The apogee of the English

George III artist's or architect's table with adjustable lifting top with pull-out drawer, with front legs decorated with blind fretwork in the Gothic manner, ca. 1760.

rococo was reached in the works of Thomas Johnson, master carver and ambitious designer, who loosed a powerful imagination on rococo and produced a series of designs, beginning with *Twelve Gerandoles* (1755), that gave the style a flavor it knew in the work of no other designer. His rococo-tinctured chinoiserie designs were so fantastic that some later authorities declared that they could never have been produced in wood. This was a premature opinion that was fortunately disproved by the discovery of several articles that correspond almost exactly with the published designs of Johnson.

Strongly influenced by French designers—most probably Francois Cuvillies, Jean Berain, Daniel Marot, and especially Jean Bernard Honoré Turreau, who was known as Bernard Toro—Johnson did not hesitate to dedicate his 1758 *Collection of Designs* to William, Lord Blakeney, "Grand President of the Laudable Association of Antigallicans." With this dedication Johnson was indulging his resentment against purveyors of French papier-mâché, which he saw as a threat to the livelihood of English carvers since it was relatively cheap, tough, and was becoming quite popular for many articles of furniture, especially picture frames.

Meissonnier, who had played so important a role in the spread of French rococo across Europe, continued to influence younger English cabinetmakers like John Linnell, whose lively, fanciful furniture designs showed that he fully understood the spirit of French rococo. Fashion, however, as it is always prone to do, tired of rococo and began its banishment less than twenty years after its initial acceptance in England. By the early 1760s, the best cabinetmakers in London were looking with interest at the fresh neoclassicism of Robert Adam, then just launched on his meteoric architectural career.

Although Adam's font of inspiration had been ancient Rome, France played at least some role in the development of English neoclassicism. The style had hit France at about the same time or possibly even slightly before it had reached England through Adam; a controversy continues regarding which country saw its first appearance. It was about 1760 that Jean-Francois Oeben, an ébéniste, led the return to the use of the straight line in French furniture, heralding a return to the classical. The close ties that leading London cabinetmakers maintained with Paris ensured that there would be a continual interchange of ideas and techniques, so the European origin of the new neoclassicism remains a moot point. It has, on the other hand, been generally conceded that rococo went out in England when George III became king in 1760.

Even after the demise of rococo, French styles continued to influence English furniture design. The paramount proof of this influence was found in Hepplewhite's *Guide* (1788), which showed furniture styles that had been proven·a success by usage in the decade or so before the *Guide's* publication. The large body of existing English cabinetwork from the so-called Hepplewhite period confirms the elegant French character of much of the best furniture from 1770 to 1785. Several of the French–style designs in the *Guide* were very reminiscent of examples of French furniture of the mid-century. This furniture tended to be rounded, graceful, and give a light effect.

Not everyone in England, of course, liked the French styles. Apart from the organized antigallicans, there were people like John Byng, that inveterate but lovable traveling snoop and a most individualistic and unorganized antigallican, who in his travels about England in the 1780s and 1790s missed few opportunities to rail against the "gaudy," "frippery," and "vile" French furniture that he found in venerable English homesteads.

Architectural designer Henry Holland, not prone to gaudiness and most certainly not to "frippery," propounded an English version of the more-serious styles, especially that of the "Directoire." Even Holland, who employed French craftsmen, never merely copied French styles, but gave all his furniture designs a decidedly English spirit.

The English designers' dependence on France did not end with Holland but continued with Thomas Sheraton who—like Holland—appreciated the more-severe French styles of the last decades of the century. Sheraton, in fact, went other designers one better by reflecting at second-hand French fads for the exotic taste. Turkish fashions were the rage in France under Louis XVI, and Sheraton's design for a "French State Bed" in his *Drawing Book* showed a strong Turkish influence. In spite of his assimilation of the French styles, by 1802 Sheraton himself was complaining of the slavish preference of English connoisseurs for the French taste.

George III mahogany washstand inlaid with satinwood, designed by James Stuart and one of the earliest attempts to create furniture in the neoclassical manner, ca. 1760–1765.

At first glance it seems incongruous to assess the dignified Gothic alongside the frivolity of the chinoiserie and rococo styles as influences on English furniture, yet both architects and furniture designers of much of the century tended to treat all three simply as various aspects of the picturesque and the unusual, providing a visual oasis of fantasy in the midst of the prosaic world. In the hands of masters, such as Matthias Lock, Thomas Chippendale, and Thomas Johnson, this practice resulted in a highly eclectic, even-eccentric, yet generally pleasing blending of the three styles, where specific characteristics of each were chosen to complement the others. In less-talented hands, the results could be less fortunate.

The affinity between chinoiserie and rococo seems understandable and even natural when we consider the importance of chinoiserie in the development of French rococo, but how Gothic came to associate with these playful companions is less obvious.

The key to the puzzle lies in the fact that the Gothic of eighteenth-century England bore as little relation to the historical style as chinoiserie did to the genuinely Chinese. As an architectural style, Gothic had never entirely died out in England, if for no other reason than that the largely Gothic body of church architecture required periodic atention from workmen familiar with the requirements of the style. In the early seventeenth century, however, English architect Inigo Jones had broken with the Gothic tradition, turning to classical Italian models for inspiration. After that time, Gothic ceased to be a fashionable style although it retained a sporadic popularity in less-fastidious quarters well into the eighteenth century. The craze for atmospheric garden nooks favored Gothic as suitably evocative of the properly contemplative mood.

Once again, architectural and furniture pattern books reflected the English interest in a style. The published designs of William Halfpenny and Batty and Thomas Langley in the 1730s and 1740s showed that there was a ready market for Gothic. In 1736 Batty Langley published *Ancient Masonry both in the Theory and in the Practice,* followed in 1742 by his and Thomas Langley's *Ancient Architecture restored and improved by a great variety of grand and useful designs, entirely new, in the Gothic mode, for the ornamenting of buildings and gardens.* Halfpenny's twenty pattern books were known for their treatment of rococo and Gothic elements. In the 1750s and 1760s, designers like Mathew Darly and Robert Manwaring followed the example of the architects and produced furniture designs in the Gothic taste.

As a harbinger of the romantic movement, Gothic suggested the transience of man's works, the supremacy of nature's. As with chinoiserie, Gothic had its literary explorers, the first two the highly respectable poets Spenser and Milton. Their views of Gothic differed, but between them they encompassed, as Kenneth Clark has pointed out, the two basic appeals of the style: the ominous and the religious.

In *The Faerie Queen,* Spenser evoked the dark side of Gothic so well that subsequent authors have only been able to embroider his vision:

> Low in a hollow cave,
> Far underneath a craggy cliff ypight
> Darke, doleful, dreary, like a greedy grave,
> That still for carrion carcasses doth crave,
> On top whereof there dwelt the ghastly Owle
> Shrieking his baleful note.

Entirely free of any darkness save the restful, Milton's *Il Penseroso* proclaimed:

> But let my due feet never fail,
> To walk the studious Cloisters pale,
> And love the high-embowed Roof,
> With antick Pillars massy proof,
> And storied Windows richly dight,
> Casting a dimm religious light.

Eighteenth-century English literati, including Addison and Steele, could appreciate Spenser's "greedy grave" and Milton's "dimm religious

George III carved and giltwood console with veneered marble top, employing neoclassical motifs, ca. 1770.

light," and before long had indulged themselves in an orgy of ruins, graves, and cloisters. Even Pope succumbed to "dusky caves" in *Elöisa to Abelard* (1717). "Bleak abodes" and "blasted Heaths" became, in fact, the standard settings for much poetry and prose of the time. No hall was whole without its "awful arches," no ruin complete without its "poisonous adder," "sightless Sculls, and crumbling Bones."

In the early eighteenth century, Gothic literature was spectacular and dramatic. In its essentials it was theatrical, often ostentatiously so, and was a fitting medium to spread the Gothic architecture produced by Halfpenny, the Langleys, and Sanderson Miller.

The 1740s saw a craze for Gothic make its appearance, and its complex rusticity became the common decorative gimmick of its day, which was brief, as Gothic was soon superceded by the hunger for the Chinese taste. By 1753, a writer in *The World* could observe that the Gothic fad had passed and that now "every thing is Chinese, or in the Chinese taste."

The fact that Gothic had enjoyed this vulgar popularity was no recommendation to most people of taste, who still saw the style as grotesque and out-of-date, something quite literally from the dark ages. The man who made them change their minds was Horace Walpole, son of the late political power.

In spite of Gothic's reputation in his circle as being rude and terribly middle class, Walpole conceived a passion for the style that enabled him to view with unconcern its common associations. The just-ending general fad for Gothic had, in fact, represented the more-or-less haphazard trailing off of an ancient style and had emphasized its quaintness and its somber quality. Walpole's Gothic was the eager groping of an amateur antiquarian attempting to regain some of the style's vitality and to give it the color and verve that his own personality craved. To Walpole the pursuit of Gothic afforded the thrill of discovery and the delight of improbable conjectures. Walpole used his Gothic as an intellectual plaything, a means of rising above and refuting the ordinary and mundane.

In reworking Strawberry Hill and assembling his fabulous collection, Walpole used the talents of some of the most competent craftsmen of the 1750s and 1760s. Richard Bentley's light touch was responsible for the rococo nature of much of Strawberry Hill's Gothic, as he liked the style primarily for the latitude it gave his imagination. Bentley was succeeded by Thomas Pitt, a good draftsman. Walpole liked to copy medieval chimney pieces and other architectural remnants, and Pitt was quite useful for such tasks. Gayfere, master mason at Westminster Abbey, built the chapel at Strawberry Hill, the creation most nearly faithful to the ancient spirit of Gothic. The energetic Robert Adam was responsible for The Round Room (1766–1770), whimsical and airy yet definitely Gothic. To furnish his spiritual and physical retreat, Walpole turned to first-class cabinetmakers like Pierre Langlois and John Cobb.

Although his work at Strawberry Hill attracted a lot of attention, Walpole did not create a fad for Gothic. Rather, he took what had been a popular craze and turned it into a connoisseur's plaything. Walpole's Gothic caught the imagination of fashionable folk, but most of them limited their interest to acquiring furniture incorporating the typically Gothic pointed arch and blind fretwork and reflecting the Gothic addiction to verticals. It remained for the nineteenth century to accept Gothic wholeheartedly.

The Gothic fad was peculiar to England in the eighteenth century, exerting little influence on the Continent. Even in England its greatest influence was yet to come.

For the rest of Europe, France may have been the supreme font of decorative inspiration; but for England in the eighteenth century, Italy was a far more important source. Its impressive classical architecture, ruined and intact, had connotations of empire not-at-all-displeasing to educated men of the English ruling class; and Italy had produced in the late sixteenth century Andrea Palladio, an architect whose published designs so skillfully captured the appeal of the classical. The wholly classical education of wealthy Englishmen made them particularly receptive to the lure of Rome, a receptivity that their travels in Italy only served to reinforce.

Palladian architecture, with its emphasis on proportion and the proper use of the five classical architectural orders, dominated English building and decorative arts from 1720 to 1750. A century earlier Inigo Jones had prepared the way for this easy Palladian conquest with his pioneering work in the spirit of Palladio.

Early in the seventeenth century, Inigo had taken a tour "over Italy and the politer parts of Europe," a jaunt that gave him the opportunity to study and to measure Italian work at first hand. While in Italy, he became interested in the architectural theories of Palladio and Scamozzi, and on his return to England referred to their work for inspiration for many of his own creations.

Inigo's successor as leading architect of the latter half of the seventeenth century was Sir Christopher Wren who, like Inigo, had a library of architectural publications, many of them on Roman and

Renaissance architecture. Although Wren exhibited a definite interest in archaeology, his work was less scholarly than that of Inigo or the later Palladians and less rigidly controlled by Roman precedent, having indeed more than a faint flavor of the French baroque.

George III giltwood arm chair with unusual ribbon decoration, in the French manner of Hepplewhite, ca. 1780.

In spite of a brief leap into fashionable popularity by the English baroque school of Sir John Vanbrugh and Nicholas Hawksmoor after 1700, Wren was still the reigning architect of England when Leoni published his English edition of Palladio's *Works* in 1714 and Colin Campbell produced the first volume of *Vitruvius Britannicus* in 1715. *Vitruvius Britannicus* was a collection of engravings of plans and elevations with accompanying descriptions, mostly of English country houses by contemporary architects (including Campbell himself). By this publication, Campbell hoped to show how out-of-date baroque had become and to gain support for a return to the style of Inigo Jones. Ironically, Campbell never visited the Italy which had provided the inspiration for what he liked in Inigo's work.

The year 1714 was a momentous one for English politics, as well as architecture. Queen Anne died, and the first Hanoverian came to the throne, bringing into power a group of young, well-educated, and wealthy Whigs. Eager to cast off the old, these young men did not overlook the potential symbolism of architecture. Leoni's and Campbell's books had appeared just in time to give them a bible, a guide that would enable them to create a new English architecture just as surely as they were creating new governmental forms.

The best known of these young Whigs was Richard Boyle, third Earl of Burlington. Young, wealthy, intelligent, and enthusiastic, Burlington made Italy the focus of his grand tour of 1714–1715 and spent most of his time there traveling about studying the architecture and forming the nucleus of his art and manuscript collection. His companion, a newfound friend, was William Kent, who had been the protégé of Thomas Coke but who had no special interest at the time in Palladian architecture. For that matter, neither did Burlington, but their indifference soon vanished.

When Burlington returned to England, he read Leoni's *Palladio* and Campbell's *Vitruvius Britannicus* and immediately recognized a personal affinity between his own artistic opinions and the architectural points of view expressed in the two books. So impressed was he that he dismissed the highly competent but hardly Palladian James Gibbs and employed Colin Campbell to adapt a design from Leoni's *Palladio* to use in the renovation of Burlington House.

On his second visit to Italy in 1719, Burlington met Kent at Genoa; and the two of them embarked on a serious study of Palladio's existing buildings, engaging Italian architects to draw all of them. By this time, Burlington and Kent apparently viewed themselves as missionaries of a new order that would return English architecture to the verities that Inigo had recognized. For most of the remainder of their lives (until 1748), the two men were literally inseparable, Burlington having provided Kent with living accommodations within his own household. Palladianism was the cause that solidified their friendship and provided them with a theoretical framework for their architectural school of thought.

In the 1720s, Burlington remodeled his house at Chiswick, employing his interpretation of Palladian ideals. In 1727 Kent published *The Designs of Inigo Jones,* which—despite its title—contained only a few designs by Inigo, many by his pupil John Webb, and one or two by Burlington and Kent. Each of them undertook other architectural assignments, always embodying opportunities for them to spread the gospel of Palladianism. They and Campbell formed the nucleus of the Palladian movement in England.

Burlington was but one of the "architect Earls" of his time. Another was the highly eccentric but versatile Henry Herbert, ninth

Earl of Pembroke, whose Palladian bridge at Wilton has often been called the most-beautiful Palladian architecture in England. Thomas Coke, later Earl of Leicester, had architectural training and certainly played a key role in shaping his monumental Holkham Hall. At Holkham, the close collaboration between Burlington, Coke and Kent, allied with Coke's vast wealth, created that strict, rather-foreboding façade that still houses some of the richest interiors to be found in England. Philip Dormer Stanhope, fourth Earl of Chesterfield, was an armchair Palladian, keenly interested in the style and its development but thinking that actual involvement in architectural endeavors would be beneath his noble stature.

But it was Burlington who became justifiably known as the arch-Palladian. His well-known passion for the style, along with his high standing with the ruling Whigs, helped to make him an arbiter of taste; and no thoughtful Whig who wanted to be considered fashionable liked to tackle a building or remodeling project without his opinion.

The Palladian movement had several effects on English furniture of the early Georgian era, mostly in the use of architectural motifs to reflect the style of building. The most-spectacular effect appeared in the work of William Kent.

Kent, a jack of all arts, was interchangeably an architect, an artist, a landscape architect, an interior designer, and a furniture designer. His furniture's massive, gilded boldness helped to enliven the sizable, if well-proportioned, interiors of Palladian houses. Kent's furniture was influenced by the published designs of Daniel Marot, whose baroque imagery was reflected so well in Kent's "Palladian" creations, and by the furniture that Kent and Burlington had seen in Venetian palaces. Kent was the first English designer to make important use of grotesque and arabesque motifs, and his furniture was successful to the extent that it created the right effect in the Palladian rooms for which it was intended.

Memories of happy experiences on their tours in Italy—not all of which, no, doubt, were architecturally or even artistically oriented—led some young bloods to band together in the early 1730s in the Society of the Dilettanti. The Society was a continual reminder to its exclusive membership of the Italian culture, and probably contributed to the longevity of the fashionable acceptance of Palladianism.

In 1736, Gaetano Brunetti published *Sixty Different Sorts of Ornaments*. Italianate in style, the book allowed some emphasis on shellwork, scrolling foliage, and other rococo motifs, natural since the

Italians had led the way as early as the seventeenth century in the departure from strict axial symmetry, the essential quality of the rococo. In 1738 Isaac Ware issued his edition of Palladio's *Works* with one of the most impressive lists of subscribers assembled in the century for such a publication. In 1740 Batty and Thomas Langley's *Treasury of Designs* showed that the Palladian influence still held sway, but was beginning to wane.

As late as the mid-century, the punctilious Earl of Chesterfield built his magnificent London home in a modified Palladian style. Isaac Ware was the architect for Chesterfield House, but Chesterfield himself chose its site in the still-rough area of Mayfair and closely superintended the work of Ware.

In the 1750s, however, the Palladian style was showing its age, understandable after its approximately thirty years of architectural dominance. It had affected not only building, but furniture design as well. Most of the best cabinetmakers of the second third of the century had followed Kent's lead in a less-flamboyant and less-expensive style that incorporated baroque motifs while retaining a basic conservatism of shape and size. It was natural that craftsmen like William Vile consciously or unconsciously absorbed the grandeur and careful attention

George III mahogany chest with serpentine front, in the French manner of Hepplewhite, ca. 1790.

to proportion that were such marked traits of Palladianism. Failure to do so would have been unnatural, for even those architects and estate builders who would not have considered themselves Palladian could not escape Palladianism's insidious influence through the many books and treatises urging a return to the classical. These were the architects who were designing and the patrons who were building the houses in which the cabinetmakers' furniture had to sit. A good businessman is always prepared to give his customers what they want and what will fill their needs; and as we have seen, the best cabinetmakers tended to be good businessmen.

Yet, as the founders of the English Palladian school died—hopefully to find a classically proportioned heaven—the taste for classicism simply paused before gaining momentum once again. The pacemaker for the revival was Robert Adam, a young Scottish architect and son of a Scot Palladian.

Although Adam inherited much from the Burlington tradition, he used his inheritance to create a neoclassicism that would probably have outraged the arch-Palladian. Drawing on the riches of Greece, Rome, Pompeii, Herculaneum, and the Italian Renaissance, Adam took the spirit of antiquity and gave it novelty. Where Palladian architecture had been dignified and imposing, neoclassical architecture was gay and seductive; and the same generalization applied to the furniture of the two periods.

When Robert Adam took his own personal grand tour in the 1750s, he spent some time in Paris, whose arts impressed him so little that in November 1754 he published in the *Mercure de France* an essay attacking the then-prevalent rococo and championing a new classical style. He found Rome more to his liking and was pleased and excited by the wonders being uncovered by the excavation of Herculaneum in southern Italy. Tutoring in the antiquities by Charles–Louis Clérisseau gave him a more-solid academic base for his delight in the classical, and he enjoyed a close friendship with Giovanni Battista Piranesi, the Italian engraver and architect whose well-known renditions made ancient Rome live much more grandly in the eighteenth century than it had at the peak of the Empire's glory. Piranesi dedicated his engravings of the *Campus Martius* to the young Scot.

Enjoying the instruction of a skilled teacher, inspired by continual visual reminders of the glory that had been Rome's, exposed to the romantic vision of Piranesi, and with access to new finds at Herculaneum, Adam acted the part of the scholarly tourist par excellence and absorbed the ideas that would buttress his creative work thereafter. His enthusiasm led him to journey across the Adriatic to measure and to record the remains of the palace of Diocletian. In 1764, several years after his relocation in London, he published the results of his study in *Palace of Diocletian at Spalato,* one of the most-important architectural travel books of the century. Momentoes that accompanied him on his return to England included engravings of architectural ornaments by Pietro da Cortona and Salviati.

Adam was not the only young architect who found Rome profitable. In 1760, two years after Adam's return to England, young George Dance, Jr., wrote to his father that he was busily engaged in the observation and measurement of Italian antiquities, in practicing his drawing, and in the study of geometry, adding: "I am sure an Artist cannot spend his time better any where in the world than here, while he is studying."

Several "artists" felt the same and some, like Adam, published their findings on the ancient architecture of Rome and other "classical" countries. In 1753 Robert Wood published *Ruins of Palmyra* and in 1762 James Stuart and Nicholas Revett, whose expedition had been sponsored by the Society of the Dilettanti, produced *Antiquities of Athens.* The Dilettanti, always interested in promulgating the cause of Italian art and architecture, had begun sending young artists and architects to Rome to study. In 1764 the Society financed Richard Chandler's expedition to Asia Minor, and in 1769 published *Ionian Antiquities.* All these books about antiquities were well received in fashionable circles, and must have contributed to the rapid dissemination of neoclassical standards.

Furniture showed an immediate reaction to the stimulus of neoclassicism. By 1761 even so recognized a master as Vile was doing some work in the neoclassical style. It was as if rococo's swirls had taken George III's accession as the signal to be gone from fashionable England.

Under the tutelage of Adam and his followers, younger cabinetmakers like John Linnell assimilated neoclassicism so thoroughly that for years most really good furniture was in the style. Inlaid ornament became popular once again, and the ornament was in the classical taste—running to urns, honeysuckle, garlands, swags of drapery and husks, paterae, and flutes. The quality of this inlay in the best furniture was superb, and cabinetmakers like Chippendale, Cobb, Langlois, and the adaptable John Linnell were especially known for their competence in the neoclassical style.

Linnell, who was so much influenced by Meissonnier's designs at the start of his career, had showed his proficiency in handling the French rococo. He soon adopted the neoclassical style, being early influenced by Adam, but only after passing through a transitional period in which he combined a subdued rococo ornament with classical forms for a highly individual approach.

Leading architects and cabinetmakers of the later years helped to maintain neoclassicism's popularity by modifying Adam's vision enough to retain the style's freshness. The modification in the hands of architect-designers like James Wyatt (also known for some interesting Gothic work), Henry Holland, and Sir John Soane and cabinetmaker-designers like Hepplewhite and Sheraton generally took the form of a simplified, more-restrained neoclassicism which was positively sober in comparison with Adam's flights of fancy.

The competent way in which furniture craftsmen and designers assimilated exotic and distant influences, incorporating what was appealing to them and their clients and what was acceptable in the cultural climate of England while ignoring the rest, was proof of their high technical skill and flexibility. Chinese, Dutch, French, Italian, Gothic—without these influences English furniture of the eighteenth century would have lacked much of its vitality and variety. With them, it made a surpassing virtue of eclecticism.

8

The Intangible Influence

he best English furniture of the eighteenth century had every reason to be good. The men who designed it were usually capable and often imaginative. The craftsmen who built it were highly skilled and had their pick of the finest materials with which to work. The practice of publishing designs gave craftsmen and patrons alike a useful reference to design. The patrons who bought the furniture were wealthy and lived in an age that viewed as well-spent money for a well-built and well-furnished house. Foreign and historical influences worked to implement contemporary British design and craft traditions. The increasing complexity of the activities of the upper classes demanded proliferation in the kinds of furniture available for their use.

Thus, needs, resources, talent, and expedience combined to produce a remarkable body of furniture that remains today as one of the most-outstanding aesthetic and technical accomplishments of its time.

There were, of course, exceptions to this glowing record of achievement. Design was most vulnerable to criticism. Age alone can do no more than make a piece of furniture old; it certainly cannot change poor proportion or unhappy ornament.

In the area of poor design, architects were most often the offenders. Their basic difficulty seems to have been a failure to understand the principles of wood construction. Architects like William Kent and Batty Langley designed furniture as if it were to be made in stone. Since it is a basic tenet that design should be ruled by construction, their transgressions not only produced ponderous furniture, but also necessitated an unsound method of construction, with the result that natural wood shrinkage (not allowed for in their calculations) eventually created serious, unsightly defects in many of their designs that were actually executed.

Initial attempts to work in a new style sometimes failed. Some of James "Athenian" Stuart's first attempts in the early 1760s to create furniture in the neoclassical taste were awkward at best. Stuart was not the only offender in this regard, and at least he had the excuse of being a pioneer. Other designers simply let themselves be carried away by the prevailing eclecticism of much of the century and tacked together an assortment of decorative motifs.

Another charge leveled at English eighteenth-century designers is that most of them did not really understand the underlying principles of rococo, and comparing eighteenth-century English rococo furniture with French examples lends some credence to this claim. Some designers and carvers appeared content to graft whatever appealed to them onto their own ideas.

The great Chippendale has suffered his share of criticism, and on occasion the eclecticism of his work did border on the bizarre. His designs in the so-called Gothic taste tended to be particularly unfortunate, and the lavish ornamentation of some of his chinoiserie work sometimes obliterated the beauty of basic proportions. Chippendale was but one of the better cabinetmakers and designers who were guilty of viewing ornamentation as superficial and not-at-all integral to design.

Even those most admired of English furniture craftsmen, the carvers, have not escaped censure. It has been noted that whatever the style of furniture on which they were working or the material, they were not particularly original. As a rule, they were satisfied to adapt or to modify existing ornamental motifs rather than to attempt to create new expressions.

In a more practical vein, the furniture was not for the most part very comfortable by our standards, but here we must remember that we should not transfer our standards to another time. Comfort was not nearly as important an element in design then as fitness for purpose.

Some of the furniture was not especially durable. If walnut, it

George III mahogany bedside table, designed by James Stuart in the neo-classical taste, and surely one of the most awkward pieces of furniture conceived by a major designer in the century, ca. 1760–1765.

could be destroyed by worms. Gesso often succumbed to normal wear and tear. Marquetry and inlay were easily damaged. These unfortunate facts, of course, indicate no more than that cabinetmakers were not gifted with the foresight which would have enabled them to work only in more permanent media.

Still and all, eighteenth-century English furniture craftsmen seem in retrospect to have struck the happy mean, to have found the point of fusion between function and form. Individually and cumulatively, the influences surveyed were important factors in this success; still, we would be doing both ourselves and the past an injustice if we stop short of the intangible influence.

There is a philosophical theory called holism that contends that "wholes" are more than the sum of their parts, that two plus two *can* equal more than four. Surely the history of English taste in the eighteenth century provides an excellent illustration of holism at work, for it is difficult to account for the spirit of the century, of which English furniture was so perfect a reflection, by a simple addition of the obvious influences abroad in the land. It is the difference between the sum of these obvious influences and the resulting whole that I call the intangible influence.

Like all impalpable substances, this idea is difficult of explanation, yielding its elusive secrets better by indirection if at all. Since the men and women of the time were themselves its mainspring, perhaps the secret lies in their personalities and characters. It is true enough that the century produced some highly memorable people.

How can we fail to be interested in a time that could appreciate Sir John Vanbrugh, able to turn his sense of the dramatic equally as well to architecture as to the theater? And would it not have been fascinating to have followed Bathurst and Pope about Circencester Park as they plotted a revolution in landscape architecture?

It is still difficult to read Coke's proud, if somewhat inaccurate, inscription over the entrance of Holkam Hall and remain unmoved by the blow dealt his hopes for his posterity. And what of the hot-tempered, powerful, talented, formidable Pembroke who was so soft-hearted that he made provision in his will for the care of his horses?

The impression still lingers of the termagant persistence of Sarah, Duchess of Marlborough, who was proud that she had not flattered Queen Anne alive and who refused to flatter her dead. The warmth of paradox still emanates from the unlikely friendship between the stiff, formal, ever punctilious Burlington and his vulgar, inspired protégé Kent and in the nobleman's stubbornness in continuing to sign his architectural drawings "Burlington architectus" while paying no heed to the snobbish Chesterfield's criticism.

In spite of Chesterfield's somewhat irritating air of continual correctness, it is sad to remember his disappointment in his boorish son and even more sad to know that his beautiful Chesterfield House set the scene for years of enforced silence when the man who so loved good company and good talk went deaf. And what of basically apolitical men like Edward Harley, second Earl of Oxford, who retained their sense of party responsibility so strongly that they encouraged and patronized artists and writers only of the same party?

One character worth remembering, if only for her stamina, was the beautiful Amelia, Countess of Salisbury, who as a girl traded her coveted kisses for Tory votes and as an old woman substituted for her infirm husband at hunts at Hatfield, continuing to hunt until she was well into her 80s and half-blind and had to be strapped into her saddle.

Even now is it not possible for us to share John Byng's pleasure in the notes of French horns unexpectedly sounding through the great park at Blenheim Palace? And would we not like to hear with Byng their "well sounding eccho" cheating the years that divide us from him and from them?

In the perspective of time, the eighteenth century possesses, in spite of its amazing diversity, a certain unity which must be due in no small measure to the influence of common sense, honesty, and individuality which characterized many of the leading figures of the age—characteristics so well-embodied in their furniture. These men and women had a passion for reason and no patience with the lack of it. If their energy and zest made them overly optimistic about the future of reason and proportion, at least they themselves enjoyed their self-confidence and were secure in their artistic intolerance, an enjoyment and security quite evident in how they chose to live.

Even the least imaginative of them seemed to have an instinct for civilized living. Whatever his mental or moral deficiencies, the average man of the upper classes managed to acquire for himself a good house, fine furniture, and quite acceptable art.

All culture has an associative value wherein lies much of its charm for subsequent times. The associations of the eighteenth century recall for us today a time when men and women were on the threshold of what seemed the entrance to a new age, an age which would surely be infinitely better than all that had preceded it. The extent to which that vision was or was not realized is debatable and does not concern us here. What does concern us is that these aristocrats, the people who set the tone for the culture of the times, were exuberant and enthusiastic and as a group accepted as only natural the highest standards of design and execution in architecture and cabinetmaking.

If the continuing appeal of eighteenth-century English furniture does lie partially in its associative values, then we must not overlook the overriding obsession with beauty that played so large a part in the lives of the men and women for whom the furniture was made. Perhaps the best tribute to them and a fitting close to this study is to quote from Colman and Garrick's *The Clandestine Marriage* (1766) the words that were so lightly uttered by the foolish Lord Ogleby, words that could serve as an epitaph for much of the best of the age:

Beauty to me is a religion in which I was born and bred a bigot, and would die a martyr.

Appendix

A study like *Chippendale and All the Rest* is much like a cookbook. The list of ingredients is there, but it means little compared with the finished product, in this case a superb body of furniture. Much of this furniture has today found a safe if somewhat sterile home in museums around the world, with perhaps the most-representative collections at the Victoria and Albert Museum in London and the Metropolitan Museum in New York. A carefully selected assortment has been assembled for the furnishing of public buildings in Williamsburg, Virginia, especially for the meticulously reconstructed Governor's Palace. Many more articles have been dispersed by sale or auction to individual collectors. Some of the furniture has enjoyed the good fortune of remaining in the houses for which it was made or at least in the sort of house for which it was made.

Perhaps I am prejudiced, but the inherent beauty of the best of eighteenth-century furniture seems to be immeasurably enhanced when it is seen in its intended environment. The furniture is no less beautiful elsewhere, but when it is "at home" we can see it as an important and integral element in the underlying coherence of eighteenth-century aesthetic design.

The only way to see eighteenth-century English furniture truly at home is to go to England and visit the great houses where it still may be found. To aid anyone so inclined, I have compiled a by-no-means comprehensive list of houses that were built, altered, or greatly redecorated during the eighteenth century and which still retain at least some important furnishings from this period. Each of these houses is open to public view at certain times for a small admission charge.

Some of these houses are almost totally unchanged since the eighteenth century, and a visit to any one of them can provide an abbreviated education in stone to the enthusiast in search of eighteenth-century taste. The most-outstanding survivor in this category is Holkham Hall in Norfolk, home of the Earl of Leicester. Here you can see the architectural fruits of Burlington, Kent, and Coke brought to ripeness by architect Matthew Brettingham, Sr. Kent's magnificent interiors, including the State Rooms furnished to his design by such noted cabinetmakers as Benjamin Goodison, William Bradshaw, and William Hallett, remain intact.

Robert Adam has fared relatively well over the years, for several of the houses on which he worked and for which he designed furniture remain much as he left them, including Syon House, London, owned by the Duke of Northumberland; Kedleston Hall, Derbyshire, home of the Viscount Scarsdale; Harewood House, Yorkshire, home of the Earl of Harewood; Nostell Priory, Yorkshire, a property of the National Trust; and Osterley Park House, London, a property of the National Trust. There is fine furniture by John Linnell at Osterley Park House and Kedleston Hall, and by Thomas Chippendale at Harewood House and Nostell Priory.

A house whose furnishings have remained unchanged for two hundred years is Uppark in Sussex, another property of the National Trust. Its architects were William Talman and James Paine, and even its wallpaper is original. The furniture remained the property of the descendants of the Fetherstonhaugh family when the house was deeded to the Trust several years ago, but was left on loan to the house. Efforts are now being made to raise funds to buy the furnishings from the family to ensure their being left in the house.

Another property that retains most of its eighteenth-century decoration and furniture is The Vyne, Hampshire, also owned by the National Trust. Both Pierre Langlois and William Vile worked for Anthony Chute when he was altering his house's interiors at mid-century.

Wilton House, Wiltshire, home of the Earl of Pembroke, on which that earliest Palladian Inigo Jones worked in the seventeenth century, contains much impressive furniture from the eighteenth century, including a sumptuous group designed by William Kent. The fine cabinetmakers who did work for Wilton in this century included Thomas Chippendale.

Other houses important both for their architecture and for their eighteenth-century furniture, which may or may not be original to the house in different instances, include:

Althorp, Northamptonshire, The Earl Spencer

Antony House, Cornwall, National Trust

Badminton House, Gloucestershire, Duke of Beaufort

Belton House, Lincolnshire, Lord Brownlow

Blenheim Palace, Oxfordshire, Duke of Marlborough

Castle Howard, Yorkshire, George Howard, Esq.

Chatsworth, Derbyshire, The Trustees of the Chatsworth Settlement

Chiswick House, London, The Ministry of Public Buildings and Works

Clandon Park, Surrey, National Trust

Claydon House, Buckinghamshire, National Trust

Cliveden, Buckinghamshire, National Trust

Corsham Court, Wiltshire, The Lord Methuen

Ditchley Park, Oxfordshire, Ditchley Foundation

Heveningham Hall, Suffolk, Department of the Environment

Kensington Palace, London, The Ministry of Public Building and Works

Kenwood (The Iveagh Bequest), London, The Greater London Council

Lyme Park, Cheshire, National Trust

Melbourne Hall, Derbyshire, The Marquess of Lothian

Mellerstain, Berwickshire, Scotland, The Lord Binning

Newby Hall, Yorkshire, Major E.R.F. Compton

Powderham Castle, Devonshire, The Earl of Devon

St. Michael's Mount, Cornwall, National Trust

Saltram House, Devonshire, National Trust

Sledmere House, Yorkshire, Sir Richard Sykes

Temple Newsam House, Yorkshire, Leeds Corporation

West Wycombe Park, Buckinghamshire, National Trust

Woburn Abbey, Bedfordshire, Duke of Bedford

Information on exact times of admission and charges is published annually by Index Publishers, Oldhill, London Road, Dunstable, Bedfordshire, in "Historic Houses, Castles & Gardens in Great Britain and Ireland."

Bibliographical Notes

Like all works of synthesis, *Chippendale and All the Rest* could never have been written without the years of patient and imaginative research undertaken by authorities in a variety of fields. Although I have had the benefit of literally hundreds of excellent books and magazine articles to supplement my own first-hand observations, I found several authors and their works particularly valuable.

There are many good histories of eighteenth-century England, and almost any of them will give the reader a clear idea of that exciting, event-packed era. The ones that I found most helpful were Harold Nicolson's *The Age of Reason: The Eighteenth Century* (New York: Doubleday & Company, 1961) ; J.H. Plumb's *England in the Eighteenth Century* (Baltimore: Penguin Books Inc., 1957) ; C. Grant Robertson's *England Under the Hanoverians* (London: Methuen & Co. Ltd., 1949) ; William B. Willcox's *The Age of Aristocracy 1688 to 1830* (Boston: D.C. Heath and Company, 1966) ; and last—but most certainly not least—Basil Williams's magnificent compendium *The Whig Supremacy 1714–1760* (2nd ed., revised by C.H. Stuart, Oxford: Clarendon Press, 1962).

Although not as numerous as general histories, there are some excellent accounts of cabinetmaking and cabinetmakers in this period. Particularly outstanding are Anthony Coleridge's *Chippendale Furniture ca. 1745–1765* (New York: Clarkson N. Potter, Inc./Publisher, 1968) ; Ralph Edwards's *The Shorter Dictionary of English Furniture* (London: Country Life Ltd, 1964) ; Ralph Edwards and Margaret

141

Jourdain's *Georgian Cabinetmakers* (London: Country Life Limited, 1944) ; Sir Ambrose Heal's *The London Furniture Makers: From the Restoration to the Victorian Era 1660–1840* (London: B.T. Batsford Ltd., 1953) ; R.W. Symonds's *Furniture Making in Seventeenth and Eighteenth Century England* (London: The Connoisseur, 1955). Also quite helpful to me were Ralph Fastnedge's *Sheraton Furniture* (New York: Thomas Yoseloff, 1962) ; John Gloag's *A Social History of Furniture Design from B.C. 1300 to A.D. 1960* (New York: Crown Publishers, Inc., 1966) ; Hugh Honour's *Cabinet Makers and Furniture Designers* (New York: G.P. Putnam's Sons, 1969) ; George N. Kates's *Chinese Household Furniture* (New York and London: Harper & Brothers Publishers, 1948) ; and David Nickerson's *English Furniture of the Eighteenth Century* (New York: G.P. Putnam's Sons, 1963).

The best book available on furniture designing in this period, in my opinion, is Peter Ward-Jackson's *English Furniture Designs of the Eighteenth Century* (London: Her Majesty's Stationery Office, 1958). Many of the original pattern books have been reissued in recent years in a variety of editions, including those of Shearer, Sheraton, Hepplewhite, Chippendale, Ince & Mayhew, Johnson, Manwaring, and Adam.

Especially good for the way of life enjoyed by aristocrats of this century are Elizabeth Burton's *The Pageant of Georgian England* (New York: Charles Scribner's Sons, 1967) ; John Gloag's *Georgian Grace: A Social History of Design from 1660 to 1830* (New York: The Macmillan Company, 1956) ; A.R. Humphreys's *The Augustan World: Society, Thought, and Letters in Eighteenth-Century England*** (New York: Harper & Row, Publishers, 1963) ; F. L. Lucas's *The Art of Living: Four Eighteenth-Century Minds* (London: Cassell & Company Ltd, 1959) ; F. L. Lucas's *The Search for Good Sense: Four Eighteenth Century Characters* (New York: The Macmillan Company, 1958) ; Dorothy Marshall's *English People in the Eighteenth Century* (London: Longmans, Green and Co., 1956) ; A. E. Richardson's *Georgian England: A Survey of Social Life, Trades, Industries & Art from 1700 to 1820* (Freeport, New York: Books for Libraries Press, Inc., 1967) ; Samuel Shellabarger's *Lord Chesterfield and His World* (Boston: Little, Brown and Company, 1951) ; John Summerson's *Georgian London* (New York: Charles Scribner's Sons, 1946) ; A. S. Turberville's *English Men and Manners in the Eighteenth Century* (New York: Oxford University Press, 1957) ; and E. N. Williams's *Life in Georgian England* (London: B. T. Batsford Ltd., 1962).

While almost all of the books already mentioned pay at least

---

*Has an exceptional bibliography for the period.

some attention to foreign and historical influences on English design, there are three books that are invaluable regarding this interesting phenomenon: Helena Hayward's *Thomas Johnson and English Rococo* (London: Alec Tiranti, 1964) ; Hugh Honour's *Chinoiserie, The Vision of Cathay* (London: John Murray, 1961) ; and Kenneth Clark's *The Gothic Revival, An Essay in the History of Taste* (3rd ed., New York: Holt, Rinehart & Winston, 1962) .

Influences on architects and on patrons are well treated or demonstrated in Olive Cook's *The English House through Seven Centuries* (London: Thomas Nelson and Sons, 1968) ; John Fleming's *Robert Adam and His Circle, in Edinburgh & Rome* (Cambridge, Massachusetts: Harvard University Press, 1968) ; Frank Jenkins's *Architect and Patron: A Survey of Professional Relations and Practice in England from the Sixteenth Century to the Present Day* (London: Oxford University Press, 1961) ; Christopher Hussey's *English Country Houses, Early Georgian 1715–1760* (rev.ed., London: Country Life Limited, 1965) ; James Lees-Milne's *Earls of Creation: Five Great Patrons of Eighteenth-Century Art* (New York: London House & Maxwell, 1963) ; James Lees-Milne's *The Age of Adam* (London: B. T. Batsford Ltd., 1947) ; Nigel Nicolson's *Great Houses of Britain* (London: The Hamlyn Publishing Group Ltd, 1968) ; and Andrea Palladio, *The Four Books of Architecture,* with a new introduction by Adolf K. Placzek, a Reprint of the Isaac Ware 1738 edition (New York: Dover Publications, Inc., 1965) .

The best evocation of the daily activities of men and women of the century is to be found in their letters and journals, many of which have been published in various editions and subject to various degrees of editing and/or censorship, most notably those of Horace Walpole, Alexander Pope, Lady Mary Wortley Montagu, and Philip Dormer Stanhope, Earl of Chesterfield. One of the most-charming journals is the set of diaries kept by John Byng while on his travels throughout England, edited by C. Bruyn Andrews, and published as *The Torrington Diaries: Containing the Tours Through England and Wales of the Hon. John Byng, later fifth Viscount Torrington, Between the Years 1781 and 1794* (New York: Henry Holt and Company, 1935) . Other helpful publications were John Ashton's *Social Life in the Reign of Queen Anne* (4th ed., London: Chatto & Windus, 1893) ; John Beresford's *Gossip of the Seventeenth and Eighteenth Centuries* (London: Duckworth, 1927) ; and Louis C. Jones's *The Clubs of the Georgian Rakes* (New York: Columbia University Press, 1942) . A slightly different sort of guide to the manners, morals, and appearance of the times is offered in *Hogarth's Graphic Works,* 2 volumes, compiled and with a commentary by Ronald Paulson (New Haven and London: Yale University Press, 1965).

The single-best compendium on all aspects of eighteenth-century life in England is *The Connoisseur's Complete Period Guides to the Houses, Decoration, Furnishing and Chattels of the Classic Periods* (New York: Bonanza Books, 1968). This guide was written by an impressive array of scholars, each a recognized authority in his field, and its illustrations make it even more useful. Invaluable for a study of the eighteenth century are the sections on "The Stuart Period 1603-1714," "The Early Georgian Period 1714–1760," and "The Late Georgian Period 1760–1810."

Magazines that regularly publish features on eighteenth-century English furniture include *Apollo, The Connoisseur,* and *Antiques.*

Index

Acacia: for painting or gilding, 58; as substitute for tulipwood, 58

Acanthus scrolls: used by J. Tijou, 116

Adam, Robert: archaeological excavations influencing, 130; and architectural politics, 77–78; architecture of, 24, 57, 78, 81, 82, 93, 114, 118, 125, 139; cabinetmakers influenced by, 24, 63, 131, 139; *Campus Martius* dedicated to, 130; and chinoiserie, 114; tutored by Charles-Louis Clérisseau. 130; competitors to, 24, 44; in France, 130; furniture designed by, 24, 57, 93, 99, 132; and Gothic at Strawberry Hill, 125; at Harewood House, 139; interior decoration theories of, 24, 114, 125; in Italy, 24, 118, 130–31; at Kedleston Hall, 78, 82, 139; at Kenwood House, 93; neoclassicism of, 24, 46, 57, 78, 120, 130–32; at Nostell Priory, 139; at Osterley Park, 114, 139; *Palace of Diocletian at Spalato*, 131; influenced by Palladianism, 24, 130; and Giovanni Battista Piranesi, 130; rococo opposed by, 130; at Syon House, 139

Addison, Joseph, 123

Advertising by furniture craftsmen: furniture design books as, 25–26, 37, 40, 44, 48–49; labels as, 21; through showrooms, 26–28; on trade cards, 21, 64, 68

Age of Mahogany, 50, 53–54

Age of Walnut, 50, 53–54

Agriculture: and Enclosure Acts, 15, 18, 85; experiments improving, 85–86; as source of wealth, 18, 83, 85–86

Alkin, Selferin: as carver of chairs made by Vile & Cobb, 33

Althorp, Northamptonshire, 140; cost of remodeling, 83

Ancient Architecture Restored and Improved by a Great Variety of Grand and Useful Designs, Entirely New, In The Gothic Mode, For The Ornamenting of Buildings and Gardens (Langley Brothers) , 122

Ancient Masonry Both in the Theory and in the Practice (B. Langley) : Gothic in, 122

Anglo-Indian style: bureau bookcase in, 59

Anne, Queen: death of, 18, 126; furniture from reign of, 23, 52, 90, 92, 109; and gambling, 98; and Sarah, Duchess of Marlborough, 136

Anson, George, Baron: world voyage of, 115

Antigallicans, 113, 119–20

Antiquities of Athens (Stuart and Revett) : and Society of the Dilettanti, 131

Antony House, Cornwall, 140

Apprentices: to John Channon, 31; to Thomas Chippendale, 31; fees paid by, 31; in France, 32–33; Ince & Mayhew as, 32; influenced by masters, 22, 49; to George Seddon, 26

Arabesque motifs: used by William Kent, 128

Archaeological excavations: as neoclassical design influence, 130

Architects: as authors, 79–80, 118, 122, 129, 139; as furniture designers, 22–24, 35, 40,